Reversing the Gaze

OVOI

Other Voices of Italy: Italian and Transnational Texts in Translation

Editors: Alessandro Vettori, Sandra Waters, Eilis Kierans

This series presents texts of any genre originally written in Italian with the aim of introducing new or past authors, who have until now been marginalized, to an English-speaking readership. It also highlights contemporary transnational authors as well as writers who have never been translated or who were translated in the past but need a new translation. The series focuses on the translator as a crucial figure for the dissemination of art and knowledge, increasing the appreciation of translation as an art form that enhances cultural diversity.

The current book encompasses all of these qualities and thus is the perfect text to launch the series. It was written by a transnational author who learned Italian after she arrived in Italy in her twenties and was published at the beginning of her career in 2001. It has been out of print in the original for the past few years and has never been available to an English-speaking audience until now. Its translation is the fruit of a collaboration between two academic women who have devoted part of their scholarly careers to the art of translation. The subject matter of *Reversing the Gaze: What If the Other Were You?* speaks of marginalization, exclusion, and, eventually, inclusion. Its publication comes at a time that beckons a reevaluation of the text, however, with a new revised edition of the Italian original and a documentary film on the author that are both coming out in 2022. We are grateful and elated to publish it as the first volume of our new series!

Reversing the Gaze

What If the Other Were You?

GENEVIÈVE MAKAPING

Edited by Simone Brioni

Translated by Giovanna Bellesia Contuzzi
and Victoria Offredi Poletto

Rutgers University Press

New Brunswick, Camden, and Newark, New Jersey

London and Oxford, UK

Rutgers University Press is a department of Rutgers, The State University of New Jersey, one of the leading public research universities in the nation. By publishing worldwide, it furthers the University's mission of dedication to excellence in teaching, scholarship, research, and clinical care.

978-1-9788-3469-9 (cloth)
978-1-9788-3468-2 (paper)
978-1-9788-3470-5 (epub)

Cataloging-in-publication data is available from the Library of Congress.
LCCN 2022011753

A British Cataloging-in-Publication record for this book is available from the British Library.

References to internet websites (URLs) were accurate at the time of writing. Neither the author nor Rutgers University Press is responsible for URLs that may have expired or changed since the manuscript was prepared.

∞ The paper used in this publication meets the requirements of the American National Standard for Information Sciences—Permanence of Paper for Printed Library Materials, ANSI Z39.48-1992.

www.rutgersuniversitypress.org

Manufactured in the United States of America

To my mother
To "my people"
To the margin

Contents

Foreword

Producing Transnational Black Studies
with an Intersectional Approach

When *Traiettorie di sguardi* (*Reversing the Gaze*) was first published in Italy in 2001, it was a unique text in the context of Italian literature and culture, a milestone in which Geneviève Makaping, Italian scholar of Cameroonian origins, articulates a complex reflection on race and processes of racialization as a legacy of colonialism and denounces systemic racism in contemporary Italy.[1] At the time, not only was there no active debate on race in Italy, but the word "race" itself was still considered unmentionable in many European countries, as it was identified with the biological category that had led to the Shoah, rather than being intended as a mutable social construction or even "social fiction" (Jacobson 1998) that needed to be scrutinized in its different incarnations in history and in distinct geopolitical contexts. Reversing the gaze of colonial ethnography, Makaping observes and records the racist attitude of the Italian population toward Black and other racialized immigrants in Italy, thus countering a long tradition in which Black Africans have been (considered as) observed objects, rather than theorizing subjects.

Makaping's postcolonial analysis is combined with an intersectional feminist approach at a time when intersectionality—a methodology that originates in the context of African American feminism and considers differences such as gender, race, color, class, sexuality, religion, citizenship, and other categories of oppression as coexisting and acting simultaneously—was absent from both the public and the feminist debate in Italy. The author's theorization is deeply influenced by African American feminist theoreticians and activists bell hooks, Angela Davis, and later Kimberlé Crenshaw, and also by other intellectuals such as Colette Guillaumin, Danielle Juteau-Lee, Mila Busoni, Paola Tabet, Teun van Dijk, Malcolm X, and Fernando Ortiz. Makaping analyzes the patriarchal structures of her society of origin—which intersect but also preexist colonial structures—and the sexist and racist approach of Italian men toward Black women in Italy (informed by the colonial imaginary of the Black Venus). She also questions the very notion of a universal sisterhood and shows how considering all women as equally oppressed by patriarchal systems allows white feminists to be oblivious of their white privilege. Makaping, however, highlights that it was white women who suggested to her the words to define what she was experiencing every day as sexual harassment, rather than just a nuisance and an inconvenience, concluding that female solidarity is a complex issue that needs to be scrutinized ("Solidarity of women? I would like to be able to study it").

The hybrid form of *Reversing the Gaze*—a written narrative with an oral structure, part diary, part memoir, part personal essay, part anthropological essay—both mirrors the complexity and versatility of the author and testifies to the difficulty of shaping a text for which the author finds no models in her culture of origin or in the Italian cultural context that can provide her with confidence or with inspiration: "It is difficult to fill the empty page, not because I do not have things I want to say, but because there are many, so many of them, and all randomly mixed up." Makaping comes from an oral culture in which the process of writing is identified with a colonial imposition ("Like me, the better part of 'my people' were brutally alphabetized during the colonial era"). However, she is determined to utilize this powerful tool she has learned from the colonizer to shape her decolonizing project and question the colonial and patriarchal structures of both her culture of origin and the culture of her country of arrival. For Makaping, the process of theorizing about race and Blackness stemming from her personal experience implies going back to painful memories: "Observing the 'others' . . . for me means observing, paying more attention than I have ever done before. It means forcing myself to bring up recollections from my memory—and not always pleasant ones—to the surface. . . . Observing means to look, to see, to scrutinize and to try to understand. Forcing yourself to look is very hard. It signifies 'self-implication.' Therefore, in a certain sense, it means to be forced not to let go."

The pain in the process of remembering results in a fragmentary text, but the fragments compose a forceful and eloquent counternarrative.

Makaping's text unfolds in eleven chapters: it begins in Cameroon and explores colonial racism as a powerful mechanism of oppression, then briefly follows the author's journey through different African countries and her arrival in Europe—France and then Italy, where the author settles—and then recounts her life and work in a small town in the southern region of Calabria and her personal achievements in Italy, including a doctoral degree. In the introduction to the text, which did not feature in the 2001 Italian edition,

Makaping from the very beginning grounds her intellectual and feminist genealogy in antiracism and Black feminism, by calling South African archbishop and anti-apartheid opponent Desmond Tutu "father" and the African American feminist theoretician bell hooks "mother."[2]

The first chapters are devoted to her life in Cameroon and her flight with Marcel, a white Frenchman who had asked Père Takala, the male authority in her family, for permission to marry her. The narrative is interspersed with reflections and considerations on different aspects of life and family structures in Cameroon. Racism is scrutinized as a colonial tool that keeps local populations in Africa in a condition of subalternity and that is systematically reinforced through representations in which white people are portrayed as morally, culturally, intellectually, and emotionally superior (when she was a child, the French nuns of the *collège* had punished her for asking "why, in religious pictures, the devil was Black and the angel white"). Makaping examines the psychological consequences of colonial racism and underlines the subtle ways in which it shapes the processes of subjectivity construction in the colonized, producing in them a sense of inferiority, which is then internalized and translated into self-hatred (Fanon 1952), a rejection of one's Blackness, and a desire to mimetically resemble the colonizer (Bhabha 1994). Makaping remembers her weekly outings to the cinema on Saturdays with the other children of the neighborhood and the fact that they identified with the white characters in the films. For them, whiteness was the most desirable trait that one could possess: "Among us, in order to say that a person was beautiful, rich, good, well-educated and the very best that there was, it was enough to say that they were white. Using French, our colonial language, we would simply say, '*c'est un blanc, c'est une blanche.*' If one of us emigrated and became even just the slightest bit successful, we would say *'c'est notre blanc'* (he is our white guy). Whiteness was meaningful." The superiority attached to whiteness in the African continent is such that, when Makaping flees from Cameroon with Marcel, her white French companion, she is allowed to cross borders between African countries (Central African Republic, Cameroon, Chad, Niger, Nigeria, Algeria) with forged documents that local authorities are not so eager to control accurately, since they consider her as "*la femme du blanc*": "Evidently being 'the white man's woman' was as good as an entry visa."

Makaping is unaware of colonial racism and its mechanisms at the time; however, once she arrives in France and later in Italy and witnesses European racism against African migrants, she begins to denounce contemporary racism as a legacy of colonialism. The education she acquires in Italy—where she gains a high school diploma, a master's degree, and a PhD—and her personal experience provide her with the tools to recognize racism and reveal its presence not only in its blatant and violent manifestations, but also in its most insidious aspects:

> Racism is so profoundly structural as to appear natural. It generates many injustices that no one has the right to commit. It is essential that we be aware of the things that surround us in order to make choices, either good or bad. One must be aware of racism, prejudice, preconceptions, discrimination, nonviolence, the hateful and hypocritical concept of tolerance and stereotypes. What I mean is that the oppressed and/or the oppressor are not necessarily good or bad by "nature." At the same time, powerless and aware, I realize that racisms seem to be increasing in strength. They seem, paradoxically, to have almost a

"right" to exist; all the more reason why it is therefore necessary to deconstruct and eradicate them.

As a strategy to eradicate racism, Makaping underlines the importance of creating and corroborating imaginaries that go beyond stereotypes and do not confine Black migrants and Black people in general to subaltern roles. Makaping claims her right to authorship: "I belong to that minority that has often been offended and, as a consequence, is also angry and often disgusted, but which also stubbornly refuses to despair. But I say nothing and I think. I think and say nothing, convinced that one day I will speak up. Where? Now, here and now. First, I shall take the stand: it's my turn to speak." Before she can exercise such a right, she needs to establish her positionality and assert her subjectivity ("I want to be the one to say what I should be called") by reclaiming for herself the name Père Takala had given her years before: MAKAPING, "'the woman who does not accept,' 'the woman who says no'." Claiming her ancestral name is part of her strategy to reconnect with her past, her family, her genealogy, her continent, in order to be able to then project herself into the future. Her assertion that she wants to be called "*Negra*" rather than "woman of color," based on the resignification of the word "Negro" (following Malcolm X), reveals the author's awareness of the fact that in order to appropriate one's story of oppression, one has to be able to decolonize and resignify the language of structural racism, historically one of the most powerful instruments in the hands of the colonizers (Ngũgĩ 1986).

Makaping conducts her ethnographic and anthropological study through participant observation focusing on her own everyday experiences of both blatant and latent racism. She presents as case studies what she calls "small acts of everyday racism," denouncing that racism is pervasive, not necessarily intentional, and that it is crucial to expose it as such, even when it is disguised as a laudatory statement (*"They* have beautiful bodies"; "Your people are better") or as an apparently neutral one ("Jenny, dark colors don't suit you"). Like Philomena Essed before her (1990), who gave voice to exclusively Black women (Surinamese women in the Netherlands and African American women in the United States) to analyze how their daily interaction with white people was characterized by the pervasiveness of structural racism, Makaping understands the importance of denouncing everyday racism intersected with everyday sexism, which in her case includes episodes of sexual harassment—both in the streets and in the workplace, both from complete strangers and from her male professors in the university environment—racist and patriarchal attitudes, the exoticization of her body in particular and of African female bodies in general, the reproduction of stereotypes that erase her intellectual brilliance and reduce her to a hypersexualized body. Through a reversal of the gaze, Makaping as a Black woman positions herself as an active observer and considers Italian "white" people as her object of observation. Makaping, however, does not conduct her research from a position of power, and yet her methodology—reminiscent of colonial ethnography with African populations—unveils the subtle (and not so subtle) racist mechanisms in postcolonial contemporary societies. The knowledge that she produces as a Black woman contributes to providing Black migrants and in general Black people in Italy and elsewhere with tools through which they can uncover their own counterhistory and create their own counterculture.

By deploying an intersectional methodology, Makaping acknowledges that the marginality of Black women exceeds that of white women and Black men because their marginalization depends on the intersection of two categories of oppression: gender and race/color. In the 2001 edition of *Traiettorie*, Makaping deploys an intersectional perspective, but it is only in the second Italian edition (2022), from which *Reversing* is translated, that she also utilizes the term "intersectionality" and explicitly pays tribute to Crenshaw for coining it. She thus recognizes the importance of creating a specific frame of analysis and a specific term that identifies the simultaneous coexistence of different categories of oppression. As Crenshaw states, "Where there's no name for a problem, you can't see a problem, and when you can't see a problem, you pretty much can't solve it" (Crenshaw 2016, 8:30). Makaping quotes Crenshaw's explanation of what intersectionality is (and is not) and of what it does: "It is not a mechanism to turn white men into the new pariahs. It's basically a lens, a prism, for seeing the way in which various forms of inequality often operate together and exacerbate each other. We tend to talk about race inequality as separate from inequality based on gender, class, sexuality or immigrant status. What's often missing is how some people are subject to all of these, and the experience is not just the sum of its parts" (Steinmetz, 2020, n.p.). Makaping's condemnation of structural racism and its intersection with sexism is here reinforced by her questioning of the very notion of universal sisterhood, strongly advocated by white feminists, and highlights how claiming that all women are equal obliterates white privilege and the fact that the relationship of white women and Black women can be one of "sisterarchy" (Nzegwu 2003) rather than sisterhood.

Reversing the Gaze is a milestone in the Italian culture also because it constitutes the first production of critical race theory and articulation of a solid reflection on racism and processes of racialization in Italy written by a Black female author in the Italian language. This contributes to decentering the United States in the context of Transnational Black Studies. As has been pointed out in different European cultural contexts (Eddo-Lodge 2017 among many others) including Italy (Lombardi-Diop and Romeo 2012, among many others), the centrality of the theory produced in countries whose racial history has unraveled within national borders, such as the United States and South Africa (Goldberg 2006) risks obliterating the role that Europe and European colonialisms have played in the construction of a global racial order. Race studies produced in Italy at the beginning of the twenty-first century have highlighted the colonial roots of contemporary racism and started a conversation on race issues, also paving the way for a debate between Black Italian and European subjects/feminists and other Black subjects/feminists around the world (Hawthorne 2019).

It is crucial that this book has now been translated into English and made available to an English-speaking audience interested in Transnational Black Studies, in Postcolonial Studies, and in promoting diversity in Italian studies (Caponetto 2021). *Reversing the Gaze* questions the very notion of an Italian homogeneous national identity and creates connections among different diasporic African subjects around the world, presenting a story that radically challenges stereotypical representations of migrants. The text furthermore encourages a conversation between race studies produced in the Anglophone world and in other linguistic and cultural contexts. This is a crucial and necessary dialogue that can, through a deep analysis of the past, allow us to envision a different future.

●●●●●

Geneviève Makaping is the first Black Italian intellectual (and a feminist woman author at that) to produce critical race theory and intersectional feminist theory in the Italian language in Italy and to rewrite the "single story" of Black Italians (Adichie 2009) being told by colonizers and ex-colonizers. Now that a vibrant debate is articulated in Italian Black Studies—to the point that in February 2022 a reflection on contemporary racism in Italy, delivered by Senegalese Italian actress Lorena Cesarini, was featured even at the Sanremo Music Festival, the most powerful incarnation of Italian popular culture—it is crucial to celebrate the artistic and cultural work of Black Italian writers, intellectuals, and artists and of artists of a new generation that includes Espérance Hakuzwimana Ripanti, Camilla Hawthorne, Angelica Pesarini, Djarah Kan, Marie Moïse, and Nadeesha Uyangoda (to name only a few) in continuity with that produced by pioneers in the field since the turn of the millennium. Authors such as Shirin Ramzanali Fazel and Geneviève Makaping, and soon after Igiaba Scego, Ubax Cristina Ali Farah, Gabriella Ghermandi, Dagmawi Yimer, and Fred Kudjo Kuwornu (the list is long and could continue), have consistently introduced and connected issues of migration, race and racism, and colonial and postcolonial Italy, thus beginning to shape a dialogue and to make a conversation on such issues possible. Literary works and films by all these authors are now available in English, and they thus introduce perspectives emerging from different geopolitical positionalities and voices articulated in different languages, consequently decentering the United States in reflections about race and racisms.

In the present context, reevaluating Makaping's work through the present publication, a second edition of *Traiettorie* in Italian (2022), Elia Moutamid's and Simone Brioni's documentary film *Maka* (2022), and a section of *The Italianist* on the making of the documentary film and on the relevance of *Traiettorie* (edited by Simone Brioni, 2022) brings attention to an author whose voice did not gain the consideration she deserved at the beginning of the twenty-first century but that has contributed to creating a cultural environment in which the themes she examines can be adequately valued and her work finally appreciated and celebrated.

Caterina Romeo
Università degli Studi di Roma "La Sapienza"

Notes

1. As the author of this Foreword, I write about race and processes of racialization as a way to expose racism, create awareness, contribute to the critical debate on these issues, and celebrate Geneviève Makaping's brilliant text. As an Italian woman who is considered white, I acknowledge that racism is not part of my everyday lived experience—although sexism is. Thus I do not claim to be articulating my theorization as part of racialized communities, but rather I consider myself as their active and enthusiastic ally in the fight against racism.

2. Both Desmond Tutu and bell hooks died in 2021, shortly before Makaping wrote the introduction.

Translators' Note

With some trepidation we approached Geneviève Makaping's text knowing that we faced a challenge that was not purely linguistic but profoundly philosophical in nature. Here was an Italian Cameroonian cultural anthropologist calling out the many forms of racism that have characterized Western society and that, in countless episodes over a long period of time, she experienced on her own skin. She was also an author who was deeply aware that language is a place of struggle. As Simone Brioni rightly points out: "Her text deals with the difficulty of translating identity, and *Reversing the Gaze: What If the Other Were You?* is an attempt to find the right terms to translate words and concepts about race and racism that do not correspond in English and in Italian."

We were immediately faced with how to translate into English words such as *negro/negra*—terms replicating Makaping's use of these words—and soon after *extracomunitari*, such a loaded word in Italian. After much discussion we decided that the best approach was to leave these words in Italian—but in italics. On the few occasions where it was used in a quote, we left it as "n–." It is important to also point out that, as with all languages, the use of the above terms in the Italy of today has evolved. (See the glossary.) There were several words and sentences in different foreign languages that we kept in the original to underscore the rich linguistic background of the author and the text.

Next hurdle: how would we deal with the standard Italian use of the masculine form of a word no matter whether it also referred to females and, in Makaping's text, challenged the mainstream white feminist viewpoint? Whenever possible, we sought out creative solutions and only occasionally inserted an explanation.

As always with the English ubiquitous "you," which helps little to convey the power play of using the informal "you" instead of the formal polite "you" in Italian, we sought circumlocutions to translate the condescension and outright racism toward the Black community and other people in the margin who are consistently addressed informally.

That brings us most importantly to our translation of the Italian term *altro*. Again, we conferred with Simone directly and, through him, with Makaping. When referring to persons in general, other than the author, we wrote the "other" or "others" using the lowercase initial letter. However, when Makaping refers to those in the margin—as characterized by bell hooks—we capitalized the first letter: the Other. The term "margin" is used most specifically: it is in the singular and denotes the place in society inhabited by all those relegated there because of the color of their skin, their gender, their sexual orientation, their "physical ugliness," and their poverty.

Final point: Makaping's intermingling of the past and present tenses when recalling moments in the past. It lends a flavor of the orality of Makaping's account that spans continents and time periods and enhances her "diary."

Along this journey we have learned much about critical race studies and are indebted to the patient help consistently offered to us by Simone Brioni—author also of the invaluable glossary included in this publication—and to the Other Voices of Italy editorial team whose collaboration we greatly appreciated. This translation was a true transnational effort!

It has been demanding but deeply enriching to express in English the strong voice of this fearless woman who has come to grips with white society with genuine love in her heart, having won her unalienable right to say:

"I want to be the one to say what I should be called."

Grazie, Maka.

Giovanna Bellesia Contuzzi and Victoria Offredi Poletto

Editor's Note

It has become almost a cliché to celebrate books we love with the formula "this book changed my life." But I really don't know how else to describe my relationship with Geneviève Makaping's *Traiettorie di sguardi. E se gli* altri *foste voi?* (2001), which has now been published in a new Italian edition and translated in English by Giovanna Bellesia Contuzzi and Victoria Offredi Poletto as *Reversing the Gaze: What If the Other Were You?* I grew up in Brescia, Italy, in the 1990s in a community with a strong presence of people from different parts of the Global South, including southern Italy, at a time in which the rise of a xenophobic party, the Northern League, seemed unstoppable. I remember having great difficulty in finding the right words to talk about this multifaceted context and its contradictions. Reading this book was one of the experiences that brought me closer to the study of literature written in Italian by immigrant authors. It also taught me that I was living in a world built in my own image and likeness, which had given me the privilege of not feeling the urgency to look for words that describe and explore race relations.

I did not find *Reversing the Gaze* an easy book to read, although I really appreciated the lucidity with which Makaping explains complex concepts in an accessible way. However,

Makaping's reflections on white privilege and injustice most radically challenged my prejudices and expectations. As Laura Balbo states in her preface to the first edition of the text, Makaping provides us with the tools to "un-learn the ethnocentrism of our culture" (2001, v). In particular, *Reversing the Gaze* invites readers to reposition themselves: when Makaping asks readers to call her what she has decided to call herself, she also compels them to take a stand with respect to a history of oppression. And *Reversing the Gaze* is a sophisticated text in which the position of marginality is continually problematized and defined with respect to gender, race, class, and geopolitics.

These complex and fluid identity articulations are achieved by using different literary genres such as the diary, the anthropological essay, and the autobiographically inspired text. *Reversing the Gaze* is difficult to classify and catalogue; one could call it a theorization on race that is expressed in narrative form. The hybrid nature of *Reversing the Gaze* could be one of the reasons why so far it has not received the attention and enjoyed the success it deserves (Benchouiha 2006, 251). Another reason could be that most literature by immigrants cannot be understood by referring exclusively to a national context but requires readers to radically reconsider what the boundaries of the community/ies are to which they feel they belong.

•••••

Some aspects of *Reversing the Gaze* are particularly relevant for English-speaking readers, such as the discussion of one's class and social status in describing oppression within a patriarchal and racist society, the reflection about language and its translation, and the depiction of racism in Europe outside from its main centers. First, Makaping's reflections on racism and sexism evidence how class and social status of a subject determine imbalanced interactions. Her writing is informed not only by original and thought-provoking theoretical reflections on Black feminism, anthropology, and postcolonial theory, but also by her firsthand experience of marginality characterized by job precarity and economic instability along with gender and race discrimination.

Second, *Reversing the Gaze* extensively discusses the translanguaging processes that are present in the ways in which migrants speak. Makaping's text deals with the difficulty of translating identity, and *Reversing the Gaze* is an attempt to find the right terms to translate words and concepts about race and racism that do not correspond in English and in Italian. Because of this reason, some Italian terms are left untranslated and their meaning is explained in the glossary.

Third, Makaping's reflections on marginality, oppression, and belonging are based on her life experience in Cameroon and Italy. She provides a critical perspective on how racist discourses have taken shape in Calabria, a region in southern Italy that is often depicted by northern Italians as part of "Africa" (Schneider 1998). Makaping places race at the center of her experience of Europe, while in Europe discourses about race and racism are often perceived as coming from abroad (Möschel 2011), and in particular from the United States, rather than being produced locally and autonomously (Hawthorne and Pesarini 2020). The new edition of *Reversing the Gaze* is animated by the desire to make the text available to readers of English who want to learn more about race and racism outside the Anglophone world.

●●●●●

In April 2021, I called Caterina Romeo to ask if she was interested in contributing to a special issue of *The Italianist* about *Maka* (2022), a documentary about Geneviève Makaping's life and work, which I was writing in collaboration with director Elia Moutamid. We had not spoken in a long time, but I knew that she had always valued *Traiettorie di sguardi*. She told me that she had just sent a list of translation suggestions to the editors of the collection Other Voices of Italy, and Makaping's volume was at the top of her list. We then decided to work together to make the publication of an English translation and a new Italian edition of this text possible. This project seemed extremely timely and important given the relevance of *Traiettorie di sguardi* to the current debate about racism and civil rights in Italy and beyond. This might explain why two colleagues, independently but simultaneously, were interested in revitalizing a text published twenty years prior and making it available to other societies and cultures through the English translation.

Contributing to the publication of *Reversing the Gaze* as an editor is an honor and an act of recognition of everything I have learned from it. I feel very fortunate to have had the opportunity to dialogue and collaborate with Makaping on a continuing basis over the past three years. Nonetheless, my activity as editor has raised some ethical issues. The role of editor presupposes an editing or modification of the author's voice through the revision of the text and the suggestion of possible changes, updates, additions, and eliminations. I reread the phrase "I must not be celebrated by those who think they tell my story better than I can" while I am writing this note in which I define how I see my role as editor. It was hard not to sense a jarring tension between the truth of Makaping's words, her description of language as a site of struggle and self-affirmation, and the task I was faced with, given that editor's notes historically have the role of somehow legitimizing the text presented. Often those who write paratextual remarks present themselves or are presented as objective and neutral figures, or worse, as experts whose intellectual superiority over the text should illuminate its peculiarities and merits. Was it necessary for me to write a note to a text that talks about white, male, and class privilege?

I wrote this note to explain the nature and origin of this project rather than to "legitimize" Makaping's voice. Her relevance as an author had already garnered attention from literary scholars before this translation was published. In approaching the text as an editor, I collaborated with the author to enhance its accessibility to a wider readership, while preserving its hybrid nature. For instance, the original text presented a sort of stream of consciousness, a series of fragmentary reflections, which in this edition have been grouped around a series of key themes. It is important to note that *Reversing the Gaze* displays an affective temporality, an intimate sense of distance and proximity to the events. For instance, sometimes Maka employs the present tense to talk about events that happened in 2001, while other times she describes them using a past tense. We have decided not to make the tenses uniform in order to preserve the palimpsest structure of the text. When Maka's voice intervenes from the present (2022), it is signaled with square brackets. A few new sections of *Reversing the Gaze* were written as the result of a collaboration and dialogue with Makaping to write *Maka* (2022). While *Traiettorie di sguardi* inspired the film treatment of *Maka*, the new Italian edition of the text and its translation in English have a symbiotic relationship with the film.

My work as editor has greatly benefited from the insightful advice of and dialogue with translators Giovanna Bellesia

Contuzzi and Victoria Offredi Poletto. The translators' important suggestions helped Makaping and myself recast some passages of the original Italian text. Likewise, Caterina Romeo read the entire text, offering generous, perceptive, and knowledgeable advice and comments. Since the production of this volume, the new Italian edition of the text, and the film developed simultaneously, it can be said that *Reversing the Gaze* has reemerged from a transmedia and translingual dialogue, which aims at sharing Makaping's thought-provoking, proudly antiracist, feminist, and transnational work.

Simone Brioni
Stony Brook University

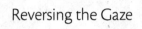

Reversing the Gaze

Introduction

My Nonaligned Feminism

Tia'h Desmond Tutu, *maa'h* bell hooks! *Po nung sî Po tï.*
Father Desmond Tutu, mother bell hooks, you have gone to
bed! So sleep, sweetly and peacefully. In my language
Bamileke, Bahuanese, that's how we greet those who for
certain—we have faith—will be part of our Ancestors made
Angels, by virtue of their actions during their earthly
residence.

I am writing a new introduction to *Reversing the Gaze: What
If the Other Were You?*, comforted and intoxicated by Lucky
Dube's music and lyrics at full volume. Twenty-one years
have passed since the first edition; a mother and a father are,
physically, no longer with us. Two pillars of my life. A pastor, a true pastor, friend of Nelson Rolihlahla Mandela, who
fought with all of his strength against one of the worst evils
of all time: apartheid in South Africa. Apartheid comes from
racism which, in turn, denies the humanity of others. And
this can lead only to the crime of all crimes: genocide, the
extinction of others by oneself. I quenched my thirst with
Desmond Tutu's words of truth and justice. Those words
invite us not to use just any means to achieve our goals, but

they oblige us to speak out and invoke love, or rather peace, at any cost: "If you are neutral in situations of injustice, you have chosen the side of the oppressor. If an elephant has its foot on the tail of a mouse and you say that you are neutral, the mouse will not appreciate your neutrality" (Tutu, quoted in Coffin 1997, 36). Tutu invited those who were against racism not to speak with their friends, but with their enemies, reminding us that "My humanity . . . is inextricably bound up in yours. We belong in the same bundle of life. . . . It is not, I think therefore I am. It says, rather, I am a human being because I belong, I participate, I share" (Tutu 1999, 31).

bell hooks—Gloria Jean Watkins at the registry office—who has eternal merit and honor for bringing the margin to the center—fed me from her breast with her Feminist Theory: From Margin to Center (1984). She taught me that "without justice there cannot be love" (hooks 2000, 39). And I, like her, "have endeavored to not only do work I enjoy but to work with individuals I respect, like, or love. When I first declared my desire to work in a loving environment, friends acted as though I had truly lost my mind. To them, love and work did not go together. But I was convinced that I would work better in an environment shaped by an ethic of love" (hooks 2000, 62–63). I too have never wanted to do certain jobs. For one thing, at the university I never wanted to make photocopies for the professors. I had figured out that it was one of the professors' ways of expressing power. Even some feminists who were "committed" to learners were guilty of this. I had spread the word that I wouldn't make photocopies for anyone, and if they needed them they'd have to do it themselves. I made that decision after one of my blatant refusals, and so no one dared ask me to do it anymore. Some friends just couldn't understand my position, which they thought was exaggerated. According to them I saw domination everywhere. But it's not like that. Where I feel love, I see no domination. Where I'm respected and people I respect sit, I see no domination.

Desmond Tutu and bell hooks had time to see the knee of the white policeman, Derek Chauvin, crush the neck of the Black man, George Floyd, until he killed him. They saw and heard his words: "I can't breathe," said in a voice that was already leaving him. It matters little whether this was a prayer or a plea. The established thing is that it is a truth. Floyd said what was happening to him and everyone saw it. That is, that this white man's knee pressed hard on the neck of the African American man—a Black man—on the ground. As if he were a worm. We all have, at least once in our life, crushed a worm, but we've never thought that it had the same dignity as us to exist.

The point is that with the term "white" we define not the color of people, but the visual manifestation of power of those who hold it, while instead with the adjective "Black," we define certain people. And we know that it's about people whose humanity is in some way denied. But dehumanizing the other from oneself—making them a worm—is necessary in order not to brand these offenses as crimes against humanity. If this were not the case, the burden of crime on one's conscience would be unbearable even for those who had to choose executioner as their profession.

"Did you kill him?" some eyewitnesses asked, while other eyewitnesses shouted: "You killed him!" Yet everyone, even the other policemen, saw the victim's head so squashed on the asphalt that his nose was bleeding. This whole story was captured live by passers-by with their cell phones, and it traveled around the world in real time. There is no other truth than what we see in those images. Desmond Tutu, bell hooks, and George Floyd have testified to those truths, and I'm grateful to them.

•••••

In the following pages you'll read my truth. In addition to Desmond Tutu and bell hooks you'll be able to spot references to some of my mothers and fathers who made me a gift of their knowledge. In this introduction, I'd like to evoke another mother: Kimberlé Crenshaw, who created the term "intersectionality." Professor of law at Columbia University and at the School of Law of the University of California, Los Angeles (UCLA), Crenshaw responded to *Time* magazine journalist Katy Steinmetz, who asked her to redefine the word "intersectionality," after too much politicalization of the term that she had coined thirty years before, in 1989, and she responded in the following way: "It is not a mechanism to turn white men into the new pariahs. It's basically a lens, a prism, for seeing the way in which various forms of inequality often operate together and exacerbate each other. We tend to talk about race inequality as separate from inequality based on gender, class, sexuality or immigrant status. What's often missing is how some people are subject to all of these, and the experience is not just the sum of its parts" (Steinmetz 2020, n.p.).

For intellectual honesty, it should be noted that bell hooks in *Feminist Theory: From Margin to Center* had already written that racism and sexism are interconnected systems of domination that reinforce and support each other. I believe that the "interconnection" mentioned by bell hooks—what Crenshaw would have generated years later, in the sociological and legal fields—was already conceptually present. Intersectionality for me is an invitation to discipline, to seriousness, because you need to be disciplined when you have to talk about the "marginality" of the Other or the other from oneself.

As a good student, I try to never forget these tips on how to practice intersectionality as a discipline, which Bridie Taylor summarizes as follows:

1. Check your privilege
2. Listen and learn
3. Make space
4. Watch your language (2019, n.p.)

I made "listen and learn" my lifestyle. And I'm still here, at sixty-three years of age, eager to get involved and to learn. I understood very quickly that occupying the space of others is exactly what we reproach rulers for, the colonizer for example, and the paternalists and the maternalists. And in my use of language I stick to what Ugo Fabietti called the "suspension of judgment" and that is "do not take for granted those ideas that tradition has imposed upon us" (1995, 25).

But I didn't just start thinking intersectionally after I read Crenshaw's and hooks's works. I encountered the works of these mothers after developing my own thoughts about these themes. Compared to other people who've had experiences like mine, I had the privilege of studying. I had already evoked this concept in my master's (1993) and doctoral (1997) theses, which were carried out with the few tools and means at my disposal. Of course I didn't call it "intersectionality," although I borrowed the concept of set theory from math in order to demonstrate how important it was to "go beyond dichotomies," especially when we talk about people, appearances, physical abilities, gender, and sexual orientation. In short, about everything that makes us different, about identities. What concerns the identities of human beings can't be represented as though it were a binary system: zero and one, Black and white, north and south, smooth and curly, and so on, while forgetting, voluntarily or not, all of the other nuances of our humanity. The establishment of these binary categories is one of the ways, even within academia, to create the concept of "race" and of racism that can come out of it.

In short, I took various paths that I caused to intersect with one another in order to show that we are many things together. I think that this attitude comes from the context in which I grew up. When the Portuguese "discovered" that the Wuori River was full of shrimp, they called that land *camarões*, and that's where the name of my country, Cameroon, comes from. Let me share a little bit of sarcasm that circulates among us Cameroonians: It's a shame that we haven't been able to go very far in terms of developing the most important infrastructures (roads, schools, hospitals, etc.) because we walk backward, just like shrimp do. We've suffered the domination of the Germans, the French, and the English. We learn all of their languages at school without dignifying our various local languages and *pidgin*, a dynamic commercial language that is evolving with young people's contribution and their ability to create neologisms. When Crenshaw talks about systems of oppression that overlap to create distinct experiences for people characterized by a multiplicity of identifying categories, she tells a story that I know well.

My experiences with "differentialisms" as a woman, *Negra*, African, poor, born in a multiethnic suburb in Douala in Cameroon who emigrated to Europe, probably made me familiar with the concept of intersectionality even before having read a definition of it. But my language wasn't ready to talk about it at all. And bell hooks talked a lot about the importance of language, code, communication, and the ways in which it's possible to express our voice so that it differs from "the one that our oppressors imposed on us," and that is, silence, lamentation, or just crying: "I have been working to change the way I speak and write, to incorporate in the manner of telling a sense of place, not just of who I am in the present but where I am coming from, the multiple voices within me. I have confronted silence, inarticulacy. When I say then that these words emerge from suffering, I refer to that personal struggle to name that location from which I come to voice—the space of my theorizing" (hooks 1990, 146).

After that she adds that "language is also a place of struggle" (146), and "our struggle is also a struggle of memory against forgetting" (148). These words urged me to speak in an accessible language in order to be understood by whomever, also and perhaps above all, by the oppressor, whatever the color of his skin. Only education and access to knowledge of the oppressor's language will permit us to speak with him. That language in that style is not useful to me to talk with who, like myself, is in the margin. We already know our misfortunes, our sufferings, because we live them and we have lived them with the forced exodus from "economic racism," at the cost of dying in Libyan jails, assaulted and raped, or drowning in the Mediterranean Sea, in the abyss of oceans that have turned into new cemeteries for those who will never be mourned. That language is not necessarily "academic"—which often means arrogant, pedantic, or educated—but accessible by who is "other" with respect to us. And it's also for this reason that I loved being a journalist. I'm talking about a kind of journalism that isn't corrupt, that turns to people in order to inform them, to expose the facts with intellectual honesty and with unmediated language. A language that is so effective that it does not need connotations to tell the truth. Just as George Floyd did when he said "I can't breathe." It's our responsibility, we who are oppressed, not only to pass on a memory by writing and telling it, but "as much as an 'Other,'" to be "a threat to black people from privileged class backgrounds who do not understand or share our perspectives, as . . . to uninformed white folks" (1990, 148).

To go beyond dichotomies means not only to talk about oppression of Blacks in the West but also to deal with tribalism, racism at the local, geographical, national, and regional levels between people who have roughly the same skin color but different traditional practices, different uses, and different customs. Tribalism is also undoubtedly racism, with all of its abuses and poisons, and it is often applied to national politics. For those observing from the outside it's not easily decipherable, but it is no less dangerous for this. It's based on the same "principles" as classic racism. It's about the negation of someone else's subjectivity or of a group of people who do not have the same ancestors as we do. It's based on the superiority complex of one over the other, of some over the others. And to Blacks in the West fighting white racism I tell them to make certain that they are not tribalists. This doesn't mean to deny in any way the concept of "tribe" in its best sense of "community," although anthropologists disagree on the meaning of "tribe." Many in the West see the denial of the concept of "nation-state" in "tribe," and often they're not wrong.

To be tribal or ethnic for me means to have knowledge of coming "from somewhere." And having this awareness is not a bad thing. Belonging is one of the components of our identity, and we need to know how to enhance our "tribality," as the pan-African philosopher Franklin Nyamsi Wa Kamerun loves to say. But this tribality becomes an absolute danger when belonging to a tribe is used to manage the affairs of a state. These tribalists of state are exactly what Kemi Seba (Stellio Gilles Robert Capo Chichi, at the registry office), president of Panafrican Urgences Movement, calls in an interview with Équinoxe TV "endo-colonists," that is to say, the African leaders in the service of "exo-colonists" who are Westerners, old colonists and neocolonialists. An example of this misinterpretation of tribalism is found in Cameroon, where nearly all positions of power are held by members of the same tribe or ethnicity—a concept I would define for simplification of exposition, as a tribe extended to others who are thought to be similar, by geographical origin or linguistic similarities.

•••••

To achieve this book I had the good luck to work with two editors: Rosa Maria Cappelli and Simone Brioni. I'm grateful to Rosa Maria who, with her patience and desire for interethnic cultural mediation (which is not only a linguistic expression), translated my thoughts in the first version of the book. And I thank Simone who tracked me down in Goito from the United States, wrote a documentary about my book, and took care of the realization of this edition and the Italian one with sensitivity, intelligence, and pragmatism. These editors did not merely share the experiences that I describe in *Traiettorie di sguardi*, but they understood them. They didn't feel what I felt, but they knew how to interpret it. They put their skills at the service of this work, demonstrating that the distance between us is not insurmountable.

Who would have ever said that this feminist text would have been published again thanks to the collaboration of a white man? But above all, what prompted him to take this operation to heart? Academic merit doesn't seem to be a strong enough motivation to me. Where does this strange creature come from? Half father—Simone has a daughter, but he's also been a father of this new edition and the documentary—and half son (a man who, if he were in Africa, would call me *Maa'h*, madre). I believe in the intervention of divine beings, in the fact that what happens is not entirely accidental. It's not superstition as labeled by the Western culture of the colonists. They wanted to dismiss our beliefs, our religions, our customs and habits, defining them as "primitive" if not outright "savage." The meeting with Simone was one of those sayings that in my language sounds like "*SI ne tchia È, E be pâ mia Æ*," which means "It's God who sent him; He is *like* me." In other words, Simo (that's how I prefer to call him because in my culture of origin *SI* means "God" and *MO* means "person") is my "eccentric twin." His age (39) read upside down in the mirror is mine (63).

Reflecting on these issues is a way for me to question what I consider to be my approach to feminism. As much as I am against paternalism, I also dislike maternalism, and Western feminists who point out a dichotomy between men and women are paternalistic. Snails, amazing beings, are hermaphrodites, neither male nor female. There are people who move fluidly between preestablished "genders," people who don't recognize, or don't want to recognize themselves by a single gender. While I've never questioned my gender identity, I feel close to how these people have questioned dualisms. There are rulers and dictators of African countries who often pride themselves on wearing a white mask in contrast to their black skin and who I see as distant from me, even if they are also peripheral to their white Western masters. There are men who I feel are closer to me even though we haven't shared the same experiences. There are some men with whom I have had a volatile relationship and who have reproached me for my normal and just "determination," calling it aggression. There are white feminists who feel they are the same as me, but they are not. I have a history of colonization, inferiorization, and dehumanization. And when I think of those who colonized me, I don't divide them up between men and women. There are feminists who have addressed me as their men addressed them. There are feminists whom I hold in regard such as bell hooks, who have never aligned themselves with Western ecumenical feminism. We were both born on the periphery and have many other common denominators, one of which is skin color. However, hooks is a Westerner and I grew up in Africa. She is a descendant of people who were deported to the United States with the *traite des nègres*, the Atlantic trade in African slaves; I was born from colonial, neocolonial, and postcolonial rule.

I am against all of these dichotomies and simplifications. My theoretical approach is that of deconstruction. I realize that I am a relativist, but this means being feminist to me. I deconstruct and I reconstruct. Continuously rethinking my position from the center to the margin: this is the essence of my nonaligned feminism.

1

The Anthropological Journey of a Bamileke Immigrant Woman

There is a deep connection between travel and anthropological knowledge. Traveling, before being physical, is a mental experience (think of the *Odyssey*, for example, or of the *Divine Comedy*) it is a metaphor for the human condition; the crossing of borders expresses the constant tension of thought that extends beyond, straddling the already known while searching for the unknown. Traveling, in this sense, is configured as an intellectual discovery. The travelers feel a typical sensation of "disorientation." They no longer recognize familiar places and shapes. In order to understand they are forced to push to the limit the conceptual tools they have at their disposal. In order to describe, they push their linguistic abilities to the breaking point. A travel report is, even more than an ethnographic monograph, an expression of the awakening of the senses. It is pervaded by the perception of Otherness from which a system of thought and writing is organized in an effort to interpret it.
—Vincenzo Matera, *Raccontare gli altri*

"I want to marry you, I've been watching you since I first arrived, I really like you."

For over a month, Marcel had been staying at Père Takala's hotel, the Hôtel des Palmiers in Douala. He was with a friend. They had come from another African country, Gabon, they said. Marcel had been watching me for a long time. Among "my people," the act of observing is not so direct, especially when it comes to asking for a woman's hand in marriage. It is the parents, close relatives, or trusted friends who observe on behalf of the interested party.

Never could I have ever imagined that the power of observation would become such an essential part of my life, that I would take up a profession where observation was paramount. It was not until many years after my arrival in the West that I was to discover that scientists based their research on the power of observation.

As a family we went to the movies every Saturday. I had often heard that kind of declaration of love in romantic films. We also watched many Bollywood films (that we called *film hindou*) and Westerns. In the Indian films we liked the grace, the singing, and the laments of the women in love. The Westerns impressed us the most. The bad guys were the "Indians," and they were annihilated. The Blacks seemed luckier; they simply served and said, "Yes, Master," their eyes downcast, and were always laughing out loud (ha ha ha!). They held no interest at all for us.

We, the girls and boys of the neighborhood in my town—a little while later I would expand this generalization to include a good percentage of Africans—used to identify with the whites. We would emulate the laughter (ha ha ha ha!) of the victors in Western movies. We would cheer them on against the "Indians," whom we jeered at from our seats. For us, it was all real. We had never heard of movie fiction. White people never cried. They did not get sick or complain. White people were beautiful and rich. Above all, they were white and that was enough. Among us, if we wanted to say that a person was beautiful, rich, good, well educated, and the very best that there was, it was enough to say that they were white. Using French, our colonial language, we would simply say, "*c'est un blanc, c'est une blanche.*" If one of us emigrated and became even just the slightest bit successful, we would say "*c'est nôtre blanc*" (he is our white). Whiteness was meaningful. Even when asking parents for their daughters' hands in marriage, skin tone was important: the lighter the complexion, the higher the bridal price. Having skin color that was too dark devalued the goods or trivialized them. "Black as coal" is an expression we used to indicate contempt. Our attitude toward white people was an "active envy." We did not want to be "them." We wanted to have what "they" had. We wanted to do what "they" did. It wasn't until later, when whitening skin products arrived from America and from France, that very many women and some young men would opt to change their skin color. I, too, tried and burned my skin. I was fourteen years old. Out of shame, I did not venture out of my house for days.

Sometimes I daydreamed about traveling. Listening to Peruvian flutes on Radio Cameroon I would cross the Andes that I was studying in school. Every Sunday morning before going to Mass, I would do the same with symphonic music, wondering how one could dance to those nonrhythmic notes. I listened anyway, out of curiosity. It was white people's music. We laughed a lot when we saw white people dancing in movies. They looked funny to us. We were convinced that they could not hear the rhythm. That is why they could not feel it—but we could. They could not even clap their hands in rhythm. In this context, our ethnocentrism was quite exaggerated. We believed we had dancing in our blood. It was a source of pride, especially since it was these very same white people we admired and envied who told us so. They told us so in the films, books, and magazines we happened to see or read.

Years later, in the West, they would tell me the same thing in person, reaffirming what we believed. Being a good dancer would continue to be a source of pride and vanity for me. In Europe, at parties, I would dance to show off. Dancing might not have been my only talent, but it was my greatest. I would also continue to laugh, watching white people dance. I did not have the tools to decode or encode what was being said or done around me, with respect to myself or to others. Paradoxically, Europe itself would later provide me with the material and tools to observe and study myself and the West.

In school we had been told that some of our brothers and sisters had been taken to America. This corresponded in part with the stories our elders told us. They said that some of their relatives had been sold. Where and when, they could not tell us. They told us that they had been sold in a distant land. For my ancestors that distant land could also have been another village. "My people" measured distance and proximity in terms of days and nights of walking. If the concept of time and space had no precise meaning for them, why on earth should we have it for ourselves? We Bamileke children were raised not to ask too many questions. We never questioned what the adults said. To do otherwise would have been disrespectful. We could only say, "I didn't understand." The elders would tell us our story, a story that always began in the same way: "There was a time," and we believed them. In my language there is no word for "time" in the sense of a precise date. I do know, however, that to indicate "a month" the new moon has to appear. A week corresponds to eight days. But I still do not know how many moons it takes to make a year. My parents do not know their date of birth. For "my people," age was meaningless. When the colonizers arrived with their habit of dating events, on the identification documents of our parents and grandparents, instead of the date of birth, they would write down a fictitious year, attributing a fictitious age to them.

Often, I thought wistfully of our brothers sold off in America. Moreover, I could not understand why if it was daytime in our country, it was nighttime in theirs, and vice versa. The thought that the earth was round caused me anxiety. I told my grandmother that we had learned about this in school. She replied that earth, as we imagined it, was flat. I even wrote a poem that I taught to my younger brothers and sisters:

> In America, it is now daytime.
> In Africa, it is now night.
> In America, the day is darkening now.
> In Africa, night is now getting lighter.
> If this is what time is, we'll never meet our brothers.
> Day chases night away.
> Night chases day away.

At no point did I ever think that my life with Marcel resembled a movie.

When he asked me to marry him, I replied he was too arrogant: "*Quelle arrogance*! I don't know the customs of your people, but it's different here. How dare you tell me these things? How dare you talk to me without an intermediary? Do you know who I am? If you want my hand in marriage, you have to go to see the 'Old Man.'"

Some greedy relatives smelled a deal. They approached Marcel offering to mediate with the elders of my family. In reality they only wanted their share of my dowry. Later, Marcel did go to Père Takala's, but alone.

The only thing Père Takala, the Old Man, asked Marcel was: "What does Makaping think?"

"She already knows," he answered.

Père Takala took it for granted that I was capable of thinking. They had a drink together. This was his diplomatic consent/blessing. He could not do it the way tradition required, that is, by calling a family meeting, making me kneel down and sprinkling some saliva on my chest, rubbing my feet, arms, body, head, shoulders with palm oil, reciting ritual fertility formulas, and following other traditions I do not want to reveal. The men would then kill goats that the women would cook with plantains. Everyone would drink both palm wine and imported wines. All bought by the suitor, as specified by ancient traditions. Oh yes, I still believe in my traditions, "those things" as some of my acquaintances or interlocutors call them. I believe in the value of our rituals, in their content and in the strength rooted in those acts and gestures. The dynamic that moves others to think of my beliefs as "those things" seems to be the same one that motivated the colonizers to call the Other a savage, not civilized.

Marcel's action broke a taboo. Pandemonium broke out in the rest of the family. The would-be mediators argued among themselves and were all against me. For Père Takala, granting my hand in an official and therefore in a blatant way to "that white man" would mean exposing me to the attacks of the family, more than I already had been. Moreover, he would certainly have attracted whispered accusations such as: "There you go, he sold our daughter and has gobbled up the money himself."

I ran away from my home, from my family—except from Père Takala, with whom I would continue to maintain a vital correspondence until his death.

From that moment, my physical journey began. A journey that would take us first to the Central African Republic, then to Chad, back to Cameroon, Nigeria, Niger, Algeria, Spain, all the way to France. And eventually I would come to Italy, alone.

Marcel died in Landernau, a cold town in Brittany, burned alive in a camper in the yard where we lived. He was a smoker. For years I felt a deep sense of guilt because I was not with him on that damn night. That night of November 1, 1978, I had sought refuge at some friends' home and slept there. Marcel had been drinking. On another occasion, while drunk, he had beaten me, and I had gone to the police. When he died, the French authorities, a police inspector and a social worker, stood by me. They took care of me. I am grateful. After the death of my future husband, I never felt I owed a debt of gratitude to France, a country I resented for having taken away my future before even granting me a present.

I Was a *Sans Papier*, Undocumented

Marcel had wanted to return to his home with me. A home that would never become ours. We started out by heading southeast, even though France was to the north. We had to keep my family and the police off our tracks in case they reported my disappearance.

That day, the day of our escape, we had arranged to meet at the bus station, the *gare routière* in Douala, in the morning. It was February 1978. I do not remember what time or what day it was. The important thing was for us to be there. In an ordinary straw bag, one of those inconspicuous ones, I had slipped my shoes and my most beautiful dress, which I had sewn myself, believing that when we arrived in the West, I should be elegantly dressed, "presentable," as they say. With us was a friend, a young man from my town who also wanted to go to France. In Yaoundé, the capital, Marcel fell ill, and I had to have him immediately hospitalized. Frightened, my friend abandoned us to our fate. I was very vigilant. In the vicinity of the clinic, I had run the risk of being discovered by one of my relatives, but I got away in the nick of time. As a fugitive, I had honed my hearing and eyesight, not out of love or desire for knowledge, but out of the instinct for survival.

Père Takala strongly opposed reporting the kidnapping to the police, something the rest of my family wanted to do. I was about to turn twenty, but I looked younger. I was considered underage by the authorities in my country.

I was illegal in Africa. I was traveling with a real document, but with fake data. From Douala to the border with the Central African Republic, I memorized a few useful things to say to the border authorities in order to obtain a pass. At my fiancé's suggestion, I recited the number of a French passport correctly: "Marcel was my 'husband' and I was twenty-three years old." Despite the fact that many of the African border policemen did not believe the document was real nor a word of what we were saying, they did not stop us. "*Ah oui, c'est la femme du blanc*," said some. Their exclamations meant nothing to me. I did not see any problem. Evidently being "the white man's woman" was as good as an entry visa. If I had no self-awareness, how could I be aware of anything else? So why should I have seen this as a *feminist* or *male chauvinist* or *racist* problem? Or, simply, why should I have worried about anything except the immediate survival of Marcel and me? Are not some women in my country unaware and quite happy to be the wife, or one of the co-wives, of just one husband?

We admired white people, yet when a real white man came along, men and women in my large family rebelled:

"She had the nerve to bring a white man into the house, after daring to refuse many marriage requests!"

"She rejected the marriage proposal of a noble and wealthy man who, what's more, was of our ethnicity."

"That girl is a rebel."

"You could go count that wealthy man's money, silly girl," some women advised me. But at the time I was studying at the Institut des Sciences Économiques et Sociales. I was supposed to become that good man's second wife-accountant. His employee. I did not give it a second thought, just as I did not think about many other things, some more, some less important things, that could have changed my life.

It was the rich man's first wife who asked Père Takala for my hand. The Old Man asked her, "What does Makaping think?" It did not even cross Père Takala's mind that he needed to talk to me about it. I was about sixteen years old at the time.

The rest of the family was outraged: "What? Women should have an opinion regarding possible husbands?"

Rumors began to circulate that Père Takala had lost his mind. Not even on this occasion did the issue of "a woman should not think" arise for me. I was not capable of reasoning in those terms, so the problem was not mine.

A year after this refusal, however, I would face another problem. From the age of fourteen, I had liked Emmanuel, a poor boy from outside my home village. His family did not want me. They said I would cost too much, given my social status. I was a luxury, and they could not afford me. All the wood that Emanuel chopped at my house in order to ingratiate himself with my family was of no use. His parents never came to our home. Moreover, they remarked that I wore pants and that I had studied too much. We broke up anyway because he got a girl pregnant. I dropped him. I was seventeen. His parents organized a nice wedding feast for him with a girl from his village. That is what they told me.

Then it was the turn of a young teacher's aunt to propose that I marry her nephew. She asked some aunts and uncles of mine. Like the rich, older man, this young teacher was also a Bamileke from my village. One of the merits of my unsuspecting suitor, they said, was that he lived in the northernmost region of my country. He used to take the plane to vacation in the village. Basically, he was considered *un blanc*. But Marcel had already started observing me, and I was somewhat interested in him. This latest refusal exacerbated my situation. My behavior, in the eyes of "my people," was unforgivable. It became the subject of discussion, of controversy and insults:

"That girl says no to everything."

"By continuing to refuse everything, she will end up rejecting even herself."

"She turned down that nobleman, let's see if she rejects us too."

Keeping it a secret from Père Takala, they called a family meeting in another town. They seated me in the center of the room. In turn, the women asked and obtained permission from the men to speak. They either criticized me or praised the young teacher in an effort to improve his image in my eyes. Among other things, to comfort me, they reminded me that I would not have to worry about the drudgery of work. Had I married someone who actually lived in the village, I would have had to take care of domestic and agricultural chores along with some co-wives. Then they gave me permission to speak.

"Fathers! . . . Mothers! . . . So, you really like this young teacher who asked for my hand?" I began.

"Yes, *gotam*, my lady," they answered in unison, convinced that this family council had redeemed me.

I turned to my mother's younger brother, whose authority was worth more than that of my father:

"Father, so you really like that young schoolteacher, of our own ethnicity, who lives very far away and when he comes here takes the plane?"

"Yes," was his curt reply.

"Then why don't you marry him yourself?" I had gone beyond all limits. I had become a river that had burst its banks.

"Never heard, never seen such things!" they said.

"We repudiate you!" decreed my relatives in chorus. I was eighteen years old. I was cursed.

God! How painful is the memory of that episode in my life! I did not cry, but I still carry the wound. With us, words have value, they mean something, they are consequential. The magic of words. For days they did not give me any food, so I made do at the homes of friends and acquaintances. With "my people," you do not have to be invited to share a meal. When you cook, the portions are not preplanned.

I was a good student. I sang and danced in the musical group at the Institut des Sciences Économiques et Sociales in Douala. I participated with confidence in beauty pageants and song festivals. When I grew up, I wanted to be first a showgirl and then an economist. People began to seriously think that something in my head was not functioning properly, especially since I constantly had headaches.

•••••

Marcel and I were now in the Central African Republic. I was not aware of the passing of time. I was not even aware of the places we were passing through nor of the people we were meeting, although somehow, visually, I sensed differences. I did not question things or people. I do not know how long we stayed in Bangui, the country's capital. I remember that one day we were prevented from entering a club at night because I was *noire*. Our Central African friend who was with us was also Black. My fiancé flew into a rage. He insulted and threatened to beat up the doorman, who was Black like us. He forcefully demanded to speak to the owner, who was white like him. They let us in. I got angry with Marcel because there was no real reason for us to go there—all the more so if they did not want us. I was unable, on my own, to think and understand that the problem was my "Blackness." My fiancé never mentioned this to me, not explicitly. If only he had explained to me, even in elementary terms, the "reasons" for differentialism—the exclusion of the Other based essentially on diversities or differences, whatever they may be—I think I would have understood.

Paradoxically, I would have understood the reasons for my so-called inferiority and their so-called superiority, given the pedestal on which, with their help, we Blacks had placed the whites. It was enough to tell me that they were rich, that they had nice houses. They were what they owned. I knew that already on my own, so the explanation did not require much elaboration. In other words, I knew the reason for their "superiority." On the other hand, I am sure that I would not have understood the same "reasons" explained in pseudo-scientific-naturalistic terms, that is, "you are inferior because you are a *negra*." In other words, I would not have been able to understand that some people could be despised *simply* because of the color of their skin. And above all, that the idea of my inferiority had been conceived long before my birth.

Our first stop on the trip was in the Central African Republic where Bokassa had proclaimed himself emperor. For his coronation, he had flowers and a crown brought from France. They say that on that solemn day it was very hot, but in any case, no more or less than usual. Thus garnered, the sweat impinged on Bokassa's majestic presence. The flowers shriveled up and only the crown of gold and diamonds held up. These were also the apartheid years in South Africa, but I was not aware of it. I did not know who Nelson Mandela was, but I knew and performed the songs of Miriam Makeba, who was from South Africa, like Mandela.

•• ●●•

We left for Chad, a country at war; I only had time to notice that many of the men we met had faces etched with long scarifications. Shots reverberated. I still did not realize that bullets could kill. But how was it possible that I did not associate those shots with the many western movies I had seen? At this stage of the journey toward the shining West, I only perceived facts that were intrinsically related to the reason for which we had run away from home. I was unaware of death and its grief, nor did I know the expressions and forms of power. On our way to Nigeria, we crossed the Cameroonian border again, this time from the north. I was terrified of being stopped by the police. No need to worry: I am Marcel's "wife." I should have always kept this detail in mind, as it would allow us to cross all African borders with ease and even to be regarded at times with reverence. Marcel was my guarantee of safe passage.

•• ●●•

Entering and exiting Nigeria. Just for a moment, my eyes register, but without questioning, the many people who sleep along the roads in cardboard boxes. It all seems strange to me.

•••••

In Niger, at Agadez, the official border, a police commissioner demanded that we verify our story and Marcel threatened to complain to his country's consulate. The officer got scared. He even apologized. And it was there, in that same town that I started to become curious. I looked around. Without asking anyone, I wondered where the famous "Cross of Agadez" was, a piece of handcrafted Tuareg jewelry that many European magazines were showcasing. I could not even see a cross, the symbol of Christianity. I would have interpreted it as a symbol of good luck. Everyone was praying, lightly tapping their heads on the ground. I had already seen people praying like that in Douala. It was normal for me. I was incapable of thinking that this way of praying, seen in all the African countries we crossed, could be considered an element of transculturalism or religious identity. We crossed the Sahara; I hated the heat, it was unbearable. Later in Europe, in the summer, I would be told, "What! You're complaining about the heat? You were born in Africa!" Marcel never said that to me. As we went deeper into the desert, he helped me cut down into shorts a pair of jeans that I had been wearing forever. I felt as if that sun was stripping off my skin.

•••••

In Tammanraset, a place in the middle of the Algerian desert, I remember feeling something close to a strong emotion at the foot of its unique, enormous tree. Maybe it reminded me of my country? Was it nostalgia? Surely, I could not be nostalgic for something I had escaped from. At any rate, perhaps that feeling (the nostalgia of arrival) put me in a frame of mind that allowed me to observe two men with curiosity. I studied them more carefully. They attracted my attention because, compared to the rest of the population, they lived in a strange house called an "RV." I got closer: they had a very strange box that mesmerized me. Inside "that thing" were people talking, moving around. They told me it was called a te-le-vi-sio-n. I stubbornly insisted that "it was a small cinema." We even watched the 1978 soccer World Cup on it. These two men, who spoke a strange kind of French, told us that they wanted to travel across Africa. They were both married. Their wives had stayed home in their own country. Had they brought them along they would only have *cassé les couilles*, "busted their balls." I was not able to think of anything that could connect those women, their white wives who "busted," to me, to us Black women. I did not even know I was "Black" before I was a woman, or vice versa. So, what had happened to all that literature on "Négritude" by Leopold Sédar Senghor and to the writings of W.E.B. Du Bois that we had studied in school? Shouldn't the primary purpose of education be to foster and develop self-awareness?

The two men in the RV had run aground because they had not planned for the sandstorms that hampered their progress. Their RV was sinking into the very fine sand. It was not their misadventure, nor was it prejudice against "the women who bust balls" that caught my attention and interest. I was violently attracted by the reserves of food they had packed in their RV: pasta, oil, tomatoes and canned sardines, parmesan cheese in the small refrigerator. I ate, but without satisfying my appetite. They had measured out the portions. I would have liked more because that pasta with oil and cheese was excellent. It tasted different from the dried camel meat and dates that were our staple. The two men were Italian. To help me better identify their country, Marcel told me that the most important city in their country was Rome, a very beautiful capital city. I asked, "Where the pope lives?" He answered, yes. Thanks to the Vicar of Christ, those two gentlemen instantly appealed to me. I immediately forgot the meager ration of *pâte maccaroni*, as they called spaghetti.

●●●●

We arrived in Frenda, also in Algeria, a place where everyone claimed to be the descendants of Muhammad. In the minibus which took us to the village, we were crammed in. I was surprised, but not annoyed, by the fact that some goats were traveling with us and kept bleating. The fact that they might be suffering did not even cross my mind. And why should I have thought so? I did not listen to them, I only heard them. I did the same with the other people who traveled with us and spoke a language, or languages, that I did not understand. There was nothing that I had to tolerate since I did not perceive anything as an explicit barrier directed at me. The only barrier or obstacle I was able to perceive, even before understanding it, was the physical one.

For a few days we were guests of some notables; we slept in their houses. It did not surprise me much that the women kept to themselves and were covered in veils. I had seen some of them in my country, so it seemed normal. However, I was very afraid and I cried when some of the men said that I should stay with the women, sleep with them and eat with them. That was the way they did things there. But at that time, I was not interested in any form of cultural mediation. I was not there to understand things. I would not have understood anyway, we were just passing through. I was indifferent to their way of conceiving the world. The urgency of my own needs was my only concern. I clung to Marcel, and he never let go of my hand. Everyone was watching us. Even in my country they would have stared at us. Men and women do not go around holding hands. Being with my fiancé reassured me.

•••••

Marcel's eyes were blue. At the beginning, I used to stare into them, trying to imagine what it was like to see the world in blue. So I asked him. He burst out laughing, but then was a bit upset because he thought I used to gaze into his eyes because I was in love with him. Then he asked me: "So you whose eyes are dark brown, do you see the world as dark?"

•••••

In Oran, a seaside town, we embarked on "Le Hoggar" for Spain. When I found myself in the middle of the Mediterranean, I felt as if I no longer had any point of reference. Africa was behind me. I felt as if I had been wrenched from my mother's womb.

•••••

We disembarked in Alicante. The Spanish policemen did not believe my document was real or that Marcel was my husband. While they were distracted for a moment, we managed to get away. The French border police did not believe in our relationship either, so we slipped across the border in Portbou under cover of night. Though I had noticed it, I did not stop to reflect on the kind-heartedness of the African policemen compared to the meanness of the European ones. I could not understand why they were giving us so much trouble. The concept of principles and rules was unclear to me. I did not even realize that I had broken the rules when I had refused marriages and had run away from home, let alone when I entered Europe as an illegal immigrant. What's more, after all, I was with Marcel.

We arrived in Pléneuf-Val-André. Marcel left me outside in the street. He went in to see his elderly parents to "prepare" them. They had no place for us to sleep. They talked in low voices. They did not look at me, they kept their eyes directed elsewhere when they were not focused on their son. I did not look at them either. "My people" do not look at others, in the sense that they do not stare at them, especially not if they are older. That would be a sign of great rudeness. Even my fiancé's brother, a bank manager, refused to meet with us. I could not understand. We found shelter at the home of a couple, friends of Marcel. I was truly bewildered when, the day before we left for our next stop—and our tragic destiny—the wife of his close friend (that's how he had introduced him to me) presented us with the bill. I just did not understand. Privately, I said to Marcel: "But what does this mean? In my country you don't ask people to pay when they come to your house to visit you!" All this was really strange and incomprehensible to me. Outrageous. It was perceived by me as a real barrier. I do not think I would have accepted as a possible explanation, "that's how they do things here."

They say that I was born on March 23, 1958, in Douala, a hot and humid city, where at a certain age almost everyone falls ill with rheumatism. My place of arrival in the world was registered as Bafoussam (in Bamileke land, my ethnic-tribal origin), otherwise it would have been like being born abroad, almost a disgrace for a person of royal origins. It is said that my maternal great-great-grandfather was king of another village. When he died, the heirs apparent to his throne, born of his expanded polygamous marriages to more than twenty wives, quarreled over who should actually succeed him. For the sake of peace, my ancestor exiled himself to what is now my village, Bahuan, in the hilly, verdant western part of Cameroon, with its mild climate and peaceful people, mostly farmers and traders. In Cameroon, the Bamileke have a reputation for being hard workers, rough, rich, and stingy.

Did I run away from home with a "white man," for love or to escape poverty? Looking back on it years later, perhaps for both reasons. Is it possible that I did not question my feelings in the face of Marcel's desire to be with me? A relative of mine, who used to predict the future for a living, had told me years before: "You will recognize your husband by his eyes, he will be the man who will take you away." And so it was. Ah, if he had been a true clairvoyant, why could he not have foreseen the ending of that story? My tears and my despair in a land that saw nothing more in me than my diversity? Did he not foresee the uphill battle I would fight to redeem myself in my own eyes?

2

End of the Anthropological Journey of a Bamileke Woman

After Marcel died, Père Takala wrote to me:

"Think things through . . . stay there, you can profit from studying and—at the same time—work. If you do that, I have no doubt you will be 'the head and not the tail,' first for yourself, and later for all of us." But my new friends said to me, "You'd do better to go back home, among your own people." You see, up to that point, I had no awareness of having "my own people." Père Takala's words, even if said out of love for me, out of compassion or pity, were perceived by me (whether consciously or unconsciously, I was unable to say) as a challenge. I could not accept Marcel's death, I could not consider returning to "my people." By going away with him, I had chosen, and therefore accepted, him and the West. However, after his death I was forced to accept the challenge life set before me.

I began to think of myself as an individual, one and alone. I had to rely solely on what I was going to be able to do on my own. A phrase kept coming back to me like a refrain, something that Marcel had said one day after a fight. He had gotten angry when I became obsessed with a pair of boots that I wanted. Prophetically, he had said to me: "*Bikette, un jour tu te débrouilleras toute seule*" (My little gazelle, one day you'll have to get by all on your own). Maybe he did not have enough money, something that had never occurred to me.

Later, in fact, I learned to stand up for myself. "*Je ne veux pas faire la bonne*" (I don't want to be a maid). I firmly told myself. I refused to be a servant and say, "Yes, Master." I wanted to be like them. In Paris, when I had to babysit a pair of twins, I demanded and won the right from the children's parents to be called *Mademoiselle* Geneviève. I demanded and won the right not to cook for anyone. I refused to clean anything but the children.

Where this confrontational attitude came from I could not say. In Père Takala's house I had seen the roles to which all the servants were relegated: they never said no and were always ready, almost standing at attention, without ever rebelling. No, not on account of Père Takala, who hardly ever saw them, but because of the rest of the family who always needed something and ordered the servants about left and right.

Eventually, I got to Italy, to Milan. I sold books door to door, envying those who bought them. Then, I worked in an office and later as a hotel clerk. I finally wanted to study, and I was able to do so. For my own redemption and that of "my people." I went to enroll at the Nitti Women's Technical Institute in Cosenza, Calabria. After inquiring about where I was from, they sent for the French teacher to speak with me. I thought we would understand each other better if we spoke Italian, "And don't just use the simple infinitive form with me, please," I said, determined to get what I wanted. I was ready to face any barriers that came my way. An inquisitive young girl, Paola Costano, who had been eaves-dropping behind the principal's door, took it upon herself to find the required books for me. I completed the five years of high school in one.

At the final exam I graduated with a grade of 48 out of 60, which I felt was an injustice since the passing grade was 36. I felt I deserved more. The year was 1988. I had stud-ied hard and, during the exams, I had also completed the French and English tests for several other candidates. On the first day of the final examinations, two teachers, a man and a woman, searched me carefully for no reason that I could comprehend. When I sat down in the middle of the other candidates, they moved me to a chair and a small table near the teacher's desk, away from the others. I did not understand why. On the day of the written foreign language tests they moved my seat again and put me back with the rest of the students. This time I understood. Racism was far from my mind. But I came to a decision: if before I wanted to know, now I wanted to understand.

At the age of thirty, I was a first-year student at the Uni-versity of Calabria. In my plan of study I included cultural anthropology; according to everyone it was an easy course. What's more, the professor was a generous grader, especially when he was in a good mood. He gave As to everyone, they said. This class opened up new horizons regarding myself and the others, stimulating an interest that went well beyond the simple grade.

In 1993, I graduated with a degree in Modern Languages and Literatures. The title of my thesis, written in French: "Integration and Disintegration of African Culture in Rela-tion to Western Culture." Grade: 110 out of 110 with honors. In 1997, I received my PhD in Multimedia Educational

Technologies and Communication Systems, with a final thesis written in Italian titled "Multiculturalism in the Multimedia Era: How to 'Communicate' among the 'Others.'"

I argued that people wage wars because they basically do not "truly communicate," they merely exchange information. People make no effort to share the context they are referring to despite meeting the conditions required by the classic model of communication. The idea for this thesis had come to me while reflecting upon my journey to Europe, when I was not interested in getting to know the people I met. My need to survive was all compelling. Therefore, the language we used to express ourselves was not important either.

After my doctorate I was hired as an adjunct professor in the department of Cultural Anthropology, teaching Sociology of the Family at the University of Calabria. I wrote articles for various journals and collaborated with the editorial board of local television networks. I held conferences and seminars in various parts of Italy. I have continued to write short stories.

What do I want to do when I grow up? I want to communicate. Once, I interpreted one of my dreams: I unscrambled the words in it and I got "Aim your actions toward the top" that I interpreted as "Always strive for the highest." I would like to be an anthropologist who specializes in communication. I would like to host a program on national TV to talk about the "ones" and the "others." I therefore want to look beyond the threshold imposed on me. Will all this become a reality? For a start, I have verbalized it, which is a remarkable step forward for someone who is, like me, *here*. "But, you know, time is passing, you're forty-two," they said to me at the time that I was writing this book, throwing up another barrier. I replied that the following year I would be forty-three, and then forty-four. . . .

And I agree with one of the protagonists of one of my first stories written in Italian titled "Nevrì Gogol and Uagadugu's Third Ear." Nevrì Gogol, a leopard who is the main character, talks to Uagadugu, an African woman seated in the audience of a circus where he is on show. Nevrì Gogol is surprised at seeing another African in that setting and starts talking to the woman about the cage he is in, saying to her: "You are confusing the cage with the barrier. There's no getting out of a steel cage, but you can jump over a barrier." Waging battle does not mean only effort; it can also bring pleasure, as well as gratification. Sharpening our gaze, even if painful, widens the line of the horizon.

[I reread these lines twenty years later. If I could speak to the girl I was then, I would tell her that I am proud of never having betrayed her. I have realized my dreams, but nonetheless I have never stopped fighting.]

3

My Not Very Personal Diary

Filling a blank page, especially when it involves *finally* speaking of the Other, is particularly difficult for me. I have never done this before. Before, I had not stopped to think, not even in passing, of what I could have considered personally offensive. Maybe I was not fully aware of it. I was totally focused on the challenges in life that were piling up. Now, to have the chance, the freedom and the right (something that minorities without power almost never possessed) of speaking out about what we had always intuited, but which struggled to evolve into consciousness, could prove to be a unique opportunity. Just like finally being able to say certain things that do not have the power to find articulation in complete and conscious thoughts—and yet they do occur—until they are completely understood. To gain awareness, it is necessary to have the means, the tools that do not belong to those in the margin.

It brings to mind a passage from an essay by Nicole-Claude Mathieu:

We must also reconsider the concept of violence. The physical and moral types of violence, the exclusion of the means of defense, the ignorance in which oppressed women are kept, as well as the "gratifications" if they remain in their place. These all contribute to the attacks on the functioning of the spirit, to the attacks on the person, to the anaesthetization of the conscience. Thus, this is what constitutes the permanent violence, the main mechanism of the domination acting on women's souls, much more than the ideal representations legitimizing the power, which are the problem of the dominants to which they also have neither the right nor the time nor the strength to access. (1985, 9)

To talk about the Other without the self-imposed limit of necessarily being "scientific"; to bring up material, even if it has been removed, in the hope that it will not cause me pain and—something that reassures me—without paying much attention to formal style. To recount and describe the facts as they really happened, as I believe they took place. After all, what is the scientific nature of a thesis if not also the synthesis or the sum of many stories (more or less similar because of colonization, racism, abuse, harassment, etc.) experienced at various times and places in the world?

For a moment, I experience a certain embarrassment, a certain fear because what I write, or what I will write from now on in these pages, will be read by others. Not because I might be judged, but because I will have to be able to assume responsibility and theoretical motherhood for what I have observed, said, and written. The risk one may run is that of not being humble enough. In a more general context, my deepest concern is that one could cut short the discourse on racism by stating that "racism has always existed among all the peoples of the world." This externalization made by an African "brother" during a demonstration against racism shocked me. I had the impression that his "serenity" depended on the fact that, since whites had racist feelings toward him and he reciprocated them, they were even. I was surprised because he spoke in terms of feelings and not in terms of exercising power. He did not seem to consider the fact that, while the "ones" could act, the "others" had to suffer, even if sharing, in some cases, the same feeling of hatred.

•••••

Racism has more than one face:

> Racism cannot be equated with aggressivity and violence; not all aggressivity is racist, and racism is not necessarily aggressive. Furthermore, racism can be laudatory; don't we hear people say that blacks dance well, Italians sing well, Jews are good at business? To define racism exclusively as a theory establishing a hierarchy between "races" is also problematic. For racism as a theory is built on the acceptance of "races" as givens, as categories exhibiting a *caractère d'évidence*. But what is this category, "race," whose existence we accept without question and which seemingly gives rise to racism? (Juteau-Lee 1995, 3)

In order to feel comfortable, I have to think that I am writing a "not very personal" journal. I have to repeat my promise to myself that I will write down all of my observations in it, that I will bring up some facts that I had previously removed without causing further suffering to myself. Because the racists and the differentialists have already hurt me. In putting out there the wrongs that I have guarded—and not even that jealously—how can I not cause myself further pain? With these statements and questions, I do not want to come across as someone who feels victimized. I am, however, a victim of the power of those who name and create labels and point to me. Victim of my wealth and my poverty, which is only the visible part of it all. My negritude ultimately seems to be here "to bear testimony" to my wealth first, and to my poverty later. The colonizers and neocolonialists knew this, and still know it well. I do not even think I suffer from the syndrome of the formerly colonized. What I mean is that I am not asking for the redefinition of the borders of the African continent, I am not asking for the restitution of anything, neither the ill-gotten gains nor my dignity, which fortunately nothing and no one can take away. I can be humiliated, it is true, but for this very reason, my dignity is, and will, remain above it all. How many times have I been humiliated, in the street, at the university, at the station . . . ? Boys making monkey noises when I pass by, while I smile thinking we all descend from primates. People flanking me in traffic to ask: "How much?" . . . I don't even ask for the cancellation of the debts that the poor owe to the rich, which is a colossal rip-off anyway. I do not know whether to laugh or cry at this last statement. Who am I? Finding remedies to some or all of these issues would not solve the problem of the Third World, nor would it solve the way people represent each other.

Therefore, I also really like the idea of considering this journal an important exercise. I think it will prove very useful as I continue to build my identity. It will be enriching. *The White Man's Black Consciousness* is the unwritten subtitle of this journal. And it is rather like a summary of the motivating factors that now allow me to write. I have given it much thought and I have chosen it for several reasons:

- Racism is so profoundly structural as to appear natural. It generates many injustices that no one has the right to commit. It is essential that we be aware of the things that surround us in order to make choices, either good or bad. One must be aware of racism, prejudice, preconceptions, discrimination, nonviolence, the hateful and hypocritical concept of tolerance and stereotypes. What I mean is that the oppressed and/or the oppressor are not necessarily good or bad by "nature." At the same time, powerless and aware, I realize that racisms seem to be increasing in strength. They seem, paradoxically, to have almost a "right" to exist; all the more reason why it is therefore necessary to deconstruct and eradicate them. The wish to build a serene coexistence and peace, however, still seems utopian.

• I want to denounce the irony, if not the sarcasm, inherent in some terminology and the cruelty of the people who use it. I speak of *The White Man's Black Consciousness* because I too am capable of thinking and making unfair generalizations. No one is without the capacity of being good or bad. What can a term mean if not the sense we give to it, granting it a negative or a positive connotation? I detest the hypocrisy that is hidden in the words we use. In any case, the term *black*, in its semantic categories, now has a negative value: black hands to mean dirty, being in a black mood to mean angry, black sheep, black heart, black conscience equals guilty, dirty "n-" (which is different from an unclean "n-"), and finally even the oxymoron black light. There are some words that actually give me hives, or close to it. The first words that immediately come to mind are: tolerance, a person of color, poor people, undocumented immigrants. These words, seen from the point of view of those who feel thus "branded," are equivalent to murder, if not in the physical sense, then at least in the ideal and symbolic one. Yes, words are sometimes stones. As I was

saying, such words give me hives, but I vehemently refuse
to let them affect my vital organs. What should I do?
I deconstruct them. I do not give them another connotation, I simply resignify them. Now you can understand
why I too, deliberately playing with words, could represent
myself as *The White Man's Black Consciousness* since I am
the victim of his abuses. Yes, who knows why the dispute
is almost always seen in terms of black and white. I do
not want to repeat here that axiom—moreover, now
disproved—according to which white equals angel and
black equals devil. However, one can try to understand the
"discomfort" of those who are inside the "black category,"
not only and not so much when one refers to the pigmentation of the skin, but when, above all, one refers to social
and political positions. So then what? I want to study
those who have made me the result of their social constructs and understand what is behind the stereotypes.
To begin with. . . .

• I want to be the one to say what I should be called.

4
To Belong, But to Which Tribe?

It is incredible, suddenly I remember that in Africa, in Cameroon, my country, the "elders" always encouraged us to write. Our requests for notebooks, for a dress or for some shoes, had to be in writing. This, I believe, was a way of avoiding or softening the typical boldness of children, the arrogance of direct contact that young people usually have. Now, years later, I also think that it was a way to improve our vocabulary and our style—our style in French, obviously. But we did this above all because we belonged to the "grand" families. "Grand" also because the real head of my family was one of the richest and best-known men in my village. He was "the son of the sister of my mother's father," my mother's cousin, seen through the eyes of the West: Père Takala. He was a cultured man. He was rich. He had succeeded in combining material wealth with intellectual and spiritual wealth. We were all his children, on a par with his actual ones.

Could it be that this exercise as "an ethnological pupil" might help me brush off part of my forgotten identity and construct another one? And how can I travel backward without losing sight of the present, the "here and now" because it is in the "here and now" that I am speaking, recalling, and revisiting?

Père Takala used to take us out onto the terrace of his modern, two-story house, built with bricks made of cement and sand, and question us. He read the Holy Bible to us. He preached and questioned us, something that at the time seemed a little odd to me.

"God is the Creator. Who is God's Only Son?" he would ask us.

"Jesus Christ," I would reply. "But Father, who created God?" I would add.

He never told me that it was blasphemous to ask such a question. With patience, and I believe, with some concern, he repeated the same dogma: God is the Supreme Being and there is no one higher than Him. In short, we could not discuss this article of faith. He never humiliated me, even when my questions could have seemed senseless. Père Takala's attitude did not disturb me in the least. I was not even tormented by many things that I considered beyond my reach, incomprehensible, like the moon and the distant stars that I often observed. Not even the sound of the tom-tom that I heard in the distance and wondered who had died.

Three years later, however, I was humiliated at the Catholic school where I went to study after I had completed my compulsory education. At a school for the elite run by French nuns, I dared ask why, in religious pictures, the devil was Black and the angel white. No answer this time. I was brusquely asked to keep quiet if I had nothing intelligent to ask or say. Above all I was not to plant the seeds of my bad thoughts in the other students. I understood that I had committed a grave sin, and therefore I was a devil. I felt deeply guilty and the following Saturday I went to confession. I was absolved

did my penance so that I was able to take commu-
 Sunday.

 ow, after so many years, almost thirty, I think that was
my first encounter with injustice, with the worst form of discrimination: racism. They humiliated me, first by condemn-
ing me and then by absolving me for something I did not
understand and for which I was simply requesting an explanation. Very probably I would have been satisfied with any
kind of explanation, enamored as I was of Jesus and celes-
tial things. Probably I would have even accepted the fact that
the devil was a relative of mine and I would have spent the
rest of my life trying not to be like him. The best or the worst
of that situation was that my schoolmates, Black like me, felt
much closer to the white nun, an angelic creature, than to me,
a diabolical one. Cruelty knows no bounds. My schoolmates
made fun of me for a long time. Had it not been for our
young age, I should have noted that I was the "differential-
ist." In one fell swoop, my classmates, Black, and the teacher,
white, formed a separate tribe: they good and me bad.
Therefore, it was a question not of color but of mindset.
I was thirteen years old. No matter what, I felt I had suffered a wrong, an injustice.

 I deeply respected and admired Père Takala. It was he
who truly "branded" me. I was about ten years old I think,
when he "renamed" me, with my consent.

 "Your name is MA-KA-PING." (He said this while sound-
ing out the syllables so that I would clearly understand.)
"MAKAPING means the woman who does not accept, the
woman who says no. MA means woman, mother. KA is
the negative particle that also implies the first person singular. PING is the verb and means to accept, to say yes, to
nod, to share. But tell me, what do you not accept? *Sing ha o
kaping ke?*"

"*Ppà ka ping potsie yie a ka pung–àa*. Père Takala, I do not accept the things that are not good," I replied without even thinking it through.

"*Gue ping, Gue ping, Tseu tsu ha Makaping*. I approve, I approve. Your name is Makaping."

My renaming was not a casual affair. As I pointed out earlier, my mother came from an old, prestigious royal family. My great-grandfather, in order to avoid a fratricidal war, renounced his claim to the throne and went into voluntary exile to the village that is now also mine. My father and his family were nobodies. Their name was not powerful enough to signify anything or, at the very most, it signified little. Mother fell for him on impulse. "Unheard of," a scandal, as one would say here! Since my name descended from the side of my biological father—it was his mother's—it was important to ennoble my name and me. And so, I spent my earliest years contested, loved and pulled in one direction and the other, because I had to be raised according to certain principles. On the one hand I learned to eat with a knife, fork, and spoon on Limoges plates in a grand house full of servants, to go out in a chauffeur-driven Mercedes. On the other hand, to eat very simply by the light of an oil lamp in a house with a mud floor. I did not miss either of these two ways of life. I did not even consider them a game; it was normal for me. Today, I believe that this going back and forth of mine from one rich family to the other poor one truly shaped me and taught me not to surrender when I reached the West, a place that very often was far from civilized.

Since the time of my renaming, twenty-three years had to go by before I began to understand the profound importance of the event. "A Negro in America can never know his true family name, or even what tribe he was descended from" says Malcolm X in his autobiography ([1965] 1992, 212).

5

Call Me *Negra*

As I was saying, it is difficult to fill the empty page, not because I do not have things I want to say, but because there are many, so many of them, and all randomly mixed up. Observing the "others," to speak of them and, in a certain way, to depict them (even branding them at times, I fear) for me means observing, paying more attention than I have ever done before. It means forcing myself to bring up recollections from my memory—and not always pleasant ones—to the surface because, alas, besides the happy ones, you must let the bad ones resurface, too. Observing means to look, to see, to scrutinize, and to try to understand. Forcing yourself to look is very hard. It signifies "self-implication." Therefore, in a certain sense, it means to be forced not to let go, while in the past I used to let everything slide off my back like a summer rain. For me, to do all this means observing and listening to myself. When you do not have "the power" that Teun A. van Dijk speaks of (1984), because you do not belong to the elite that "names" and transmits preconceptions and prejudices, the exercise becomes even more difficult. How am I to be sure that I am in the right, that my gaze is the correct one? Most certainly my ex-colonizers—and the new ones—never asked themselves this question, or if they did, they did it without agonizing about it. How am I to know if my gaze is the correct one, without question, just because I am a minority?

I belong to that minority that has often been offended and, as a consequence, is also angry and often disgusted, but which also stubbornly refuses to despair. But I say nothing and I think. I think and say nothing, convinced that one day I will speak up. Where? Now, here and now. First, I shall take the stand: it's my turn to speak. I am a minority since I am a Cameroonian within the Italian majority. This fact in itself does not overwhelm me. It could be the same for a Westerner living in my country—but with one big difference: I doubt whether their biggest problem might be not knowing how to get to the end of the month. I am not, and I do not want to be, a whining minority. Therefore, being a minority, also by virtue of the stand that I am taking, does not overwhelm me, perhaps because of my path in life, my experience and my sufferings. I have been a minority many times. It is irrefutable that minorities and majorities will always exist and the concept of them should be relativized and contextualized. Certainly not in the sense of that relativism that holds that we are all equal but that each should stay in their own place. I do not believe that difference has to signify that one group has all the rights and the other, only duties. Or, moreover, that one group has more rights than the other. The point is that, in the majority of cases, the minority has only one right: to obey. I know, I am being sarcastic. I want to have the strength and the tools to claim and take up my freedom to have duties and rights as a person. I want to refuse to fight for the right to be different, from the racial, ethnic or sexual point of view. That could mean fighting for the continuation of my subordination in that the difference is almost always tied to domination (Juteau-Lee 1995, 17).

My gaze moves from one place to the other, and I have to remind myself that I am also the subject of this gaze, moving and turning it on myself. The privilege of this kind of approach can change depending on the situation. I can be both the margin and the center at almost the same time.

In the past, to put it simply, I was not looking, or, I was looking but I saw little; I could not focus properly or, perhaps, I did not want to. It was not even an attitude such as: "Let them think and say what they want, who cares?" I do not even consider it a type of superiority complex ("they're the ones who are ignorant . . ."). It was just a *non-gaze*. If before I did not observe the "others," white people, perhaps it depended on the fact that I was not aware that they were observing me, actually, that they had already observed and cataloged me through their forefathers' travels, stories, and ethnographic research.

If I did not observe the "others," it was not because my gaze was directed elsewhere, not even on me. Instead, It was a disinterested gaze, because the others did not arouse my interest. Or perhaps, I acted in such a way so that they would not arouse it. If someone said, "I don't like *negri*," I simply thought—in French—"what's that got to do with me?" It wasn't even a question inviting an answer. I simply thought: "It's their problem, period." However, occasionally it did make me rethink what had happened, but I was very careful not to let on what I thought, even when I could have. I opted for silence. To put it simply, I could not, nor did I want to, make my voice heard. I think that attitude of mine—I do not know if or how premeditated on my part—served as some kind of armor. Was it possible that the fear of becoming involved was so strong that my intellect had built a kind of defense mechanism? I do not believe so. My choice to remain silent was a conscious one. Not an agonized choice. An instinctive choice. It is also possible that a healthy dose of narcissism helped me not to surrender to those who despise me and others like me: we who are different from them.

I am not a "woman of color." I am a *Negra*. I have no reason to feel proud or, conversely, to feel unhappy about being a *Negra*, no matter what the point of view may be. Historically, biologically, politically, socially they have tried to explain who I am. I am shocked to discover all the things behind racist theories, and I come to the conclusion that, in reality, the problem is not my skin in and of itself. I read in a piece about racism by Danielle Juteau-Lee: "It is not because your skin is black that you were enslaved, that you became a slave, but because you were a slave that you became black, or more precisely that colour became significant. . . . Colour became discriminant when a social group was in fact constituted. In other words, slavery as a system was not built on the appearance of its agents but on the appropriation of their labour" (1995, 6).

These are illuminating explanations for understanding the naturalist-racist ideology, which, in substance, claims that the significance of a sign is in the sign itself. It is therefore self-referent. A healthy mind tells us that the opposite is true, that is, the relationship between signifier and its signified is purely arbitrary, when it is not of a simple onomatopoeic origin, and is accepted for convenience's sake.

Years ago, on the Italian TV show *I fatti vostri* I saw a young woman crying inconsolably because, on a bus in Rome, a man had addressed her with the n-word. I was shocked by her tears and from that moment on I decided I would intensify my efforts for the deconstruction and reconstruction of certain concepts. The young woman was not even expecting to be identified by her name or by her country of origin, which, in a way, would have diminished the distance between her and the "other." "I am a woman of color," she implored. I thought that, if the man on the bus did not know who she was, very probably neither was she aware of it herself. "My black brothers and sisters—no one will know who we are . . . until we know who we are!" declares Malcolm X ([1965] 1992, 257).

Expressions like "woman of color" or *extracomunitaria* rile me because only now do I understand what kind of attitude and thought lie behind these labels. It is a case of denying individuality, of denying another's identity (including the visible, external one), a denial constructed for precise objectives by those in power. The majority who use apartheid racist terms is certainly not always aware of it, and therefore should not be assigned blame, but most certainly needs to be educated. I hope that I will never be disgusted by whoever says such things. I do not want to be like "them." I have to keep my fingers crossed against the eventuality of becoming like "them," now that I have achieved awareness. I have to unlearn before I can learn, and that having completed this exercise, I do not discover I behaved exactly like them, but unconsciously so. If I were to discover that I had acted like "them" and persevered with this type of thinking and behavior, it would mean that I have consciously made a choice to be racist. This will not happen.

Here the discussion becomes complicated because I have to distinguish between a racist "them" and a "them" simply "other than me." It means finding the right words. I am intrigued by those who present themselves to my eyes simply as "other than me." The differences could enrich my cultural baggage, produce a comparison and, at times, a clash. But a clash does not necessarily lead to a duel or a war, as evidenced in many parts of the world. I want to be capable of not letting myself become fascinated by the type of power that programs and produces the subalternity of the "other than me," even if out of vendetta, ransom or revenge. I realize that these statements might make one smile. There is the risk of coming off as a do-gooder, as sometimes I have heard my colleagues say to me in the various workplaces that I frequent. I had a hard time convincing two journalist colleagues of mine that the goodness of my intentions is not innate in me, nor a weakness, but a choice from the moment I refused to join their "squadron" to take part in the mobbing of a colleague. I am a firm believer in the importance of getting up in the morning with a clear conscience. I believe in the centrality of man as an individual.

Now I am forty-two years old. I want to and have to write, to transcribe my observations. But where do I observe? Where do I find the material for observing? I look back, I look at the present, I look at whoever considers my diversity blameworthy, forgetting their own. Diversities are by definition at least two. I look at whoever has considered the color of my skin a sickness, I look at whoever is convinced that I must, and can only, serve. I want to observe those who bet against me, as if I were a player in a game. *I look at myself looking at those who have always been looking at me.*

Might I be exaggerating? No. I am speaking, at peace with myself. Now I have the power of my pen, or should I say, of my keyboard. This, this is power. I must admit that it has a certain fascination. Power allows you to feel like a Supreme Being and you must be constantly vigilant that it does not overwhelm you. Humility? No, simple reason. I think I'll have quite some stories to tell, and it will not only be to vent because I don't think I have strong poisons inside me; I am not a snake. I don't have to vindicate anything. Were that the case, I would have to vindicate the entire world. I would have to vindicate all the oppressed of the world. I would have to vindicate the starving, the illiterate, the misinformed, and the slain innocents. I would have to assume the role of judge, which I am not. I cannot even believe in an avenging God. I have chosen the path of nonviolence, of reason, and of the power of the word. I want to write *The White Man's Black Consciousness* in the hope that "those whose hands and thoughts are stained" can recognize themselves, personally and collectively.

6

The Difficulty of Dialoguing
within the Margin

I have chosen to make my gaze direct; it must be able to
linger on what surrounds me. But now that I have identified on whom or on what to turn my gaze, another no less
important problem arises with full force: in what language
should I speak to *them*? Are *they* able to understand my language? The language of those who are powerless? The
language of suffering and hardship? In short, how can
the margin speak to the center if dialogue is already not a
given among those in the margin? A statement by bell
hooks comes to mind:

> We are wedded in language, have our being in words.
> Language is also a place of struggle. Dare I speak to
> oppressed and oppressor in the same voice? Dare I speak
> to you in a language that will move beyond the boundaries
> of domination—a language that will not bind you, fence
> you in, or hold you. Language is also a place of struggle.
> The oppressed struggle in language to recover ourselves, to
> reconcile, to reunite, to renew. Our words are not without

meaning, they are an action, a resistance. Language is also a place of struggle. (1990, 146)

If dialogue with the center is difficult, dialogue among those relegated to the margin is not a given. My primary element of diversity in Italy—skin color—is obvious. But there are also whites who find themselves in the margin by way of their "condition" of homosexuality, "physical ugliness"—obviously according to the Western canon—failure, poverty. Not all the people in the margin share the same goals. I also learned about the margin of foreign communities in Calabria, which merit further research. The female editor-in-chief of a private television station with which I collaborate asked me to prepare some pieces on these foreign communities in Calabria. I come up with the title "The World in Calabria." A young journalist suggests "People," which I find much more anthropological. The idea of the program is that these communities will be the ones to present themselves to the Calabrians, as they see fit. My wish is that *they themselves should be the ones to say what they should be called*. However, I stop doing these recordings because some of these communities ask to be paid. I am profoundly discouraged. . . . What does the margin think, what does the center think? What do they learn from each other?

I have a friend who often says to me, "Jenny, you and I are the same," "you are like me," "you and I are alike," "you . . . like me." I have been intrigued by the fact that, in all her statements, she has never uttered a phrase of the type "we are the same," "we are alike," "we. . . ." It is always me like her, never her like me. Even by virtue of the differences that relegate us to the margin, I always come after her. She is the active subject and I am the passive object, even in our misfortunes.

The fundamental and unresolved problem with the "great margin," on a global level, is that the "poor white person" still feels entitled to always feel superior to the "dirty n–," *of course.*

I met a homosexual man mocked by people who share his white culture, that of the heterosexual majority, who told me: "You know, Jenny, you are an exception. I just hate *negri.* I would never get involved with a black-skinned guy." On more than one occasion, in different ways, he repeated this to me. On those occasions, I really wanted to make my voice heard. I chose not to.

I carefully avoided answering because it would have seemed like a pointless quarrel between two "poor devils," and I do not feel like one. A fight between poor people, as clashes between groups of "different" people from all over the city are often dismissed. Then I would have told him that there are also Black homosexuals and that, therefore, being one is not a prerogative of whites only. I would have been mean, because, being who I am, I would have defended my conviction to the point of screaming, to get it into his head once and for all. I would have told him that I couldn't care less whether he cared for me or not, because there doesn't exist a civil "law" that requires that these feelings be reciprocated. Not caring does not necessarily mean hating. But then again, not being a homosexual, I did not see why I should have to respond on behalf of Black homosexuals, among whom perhaps some share the same racist thinking.

I now try to analyze my thinking in order to understand if there was any element of prejudice in that way of reasoning and acting. I admit that I was weighed down by ignorance, in the sense that I did not have any kind of understanding about what it means to be homosexual. There were a lot of things I did not know. In Douala, my hometown in

Cameroon, I had heard the insult *pédé* (f-g) being used, but for me, until I came to Europe, it was an insult just like many others that we children used merely for the sake of offending others. I am not at all comforted by the idea that I never linked *pédé*, the insult, to the concept of homosexuality. Ignorance should not always grant absolution.

7

The Anthropology of the Other

Being in the here and now is just one stop along my journey. It is the longest stopover. I have lived in Italy—in Calabria for the most part—for more than twenty years. This is a most important stopover on my journey as I become aware of myself, the Other, and of those other than me. As I write this diary, I am aware of revisiting and analyzing my memory, my past memory and the one taking shape in the future. I journey through my own various identities in particular, and the identity of those other than me in general.

The act of writing continues to be arduous. Can this exceptional medium be a truly effective tool for telling stories? To tell the story of my life? Writing, like Western thought, leverages a very specific time and space. Formal grammar is one such example. Syntax is another.

I come from a part of the world where, until recently, oral culture was the norm. Like me, the better part of "my people" were brutally alphabetized during the colonial era. I was not prepared to be alphabetized. My mother nursed me until I was five; I remember it well. I liked it. The following year I found myself turned out and sitting under a tree where a man reproduced strange signs with a piece of chalk on a blackboard hanging from a branch. We had to transcribe those signs and pronounce them correctly. The teacher would hit us if we failed at the first try. It was far from pleasant to be castigated because we were not immediately able to learn something that should have been for our benefit. We were stunned. In the class under the tree there were many of us children. We came from at least twenty different ethnic groups, and each of us spoke our own mother tongue.

I am not challenging the idea of writing, I am only protesting against its decontextualization. In order for us to better understand who we were, the act of alphabetization should have sought to tell us this in our own language. First of all, it should have linked those signs to the things we all knew and saw. Writing calls for a certain linearity that does not always correspond, synchronically and diachronically, to the different rhythms of life of those who live in an oral culture. I have chosen to write this diary because leaving Cameroon signified not only moving myself in space, but also, in some ways, breaking down the barrier of time. Noting down the stages along the way as I cross spatial, temporal, and mental barriers serves to put into place some "signs" that help me to preserve, to understand a part of the things that happened to me and that continue to happen to me every day. It helps me to better recollect certain facts and, at the same time, to forget others.

•••••

Often, on my journey, there was nobody to share with, to speak to, nobody to listen to me. To converse with. To be listened to, to be understood is an extraordinary experience.

Saturday, July 15, 2000: I was on the train to Naples. I was absorbed in reading a book that presented me with a series

of thoughts such as: Oh, look, Geneviève, you're not a
just because your sex is anatomically different from
the male. C'mon, think about it! The sex you were sthas to do with power, politics, and social change. In a nasn,
I realized that, before me, was a much more important issue
than I was capable of facing and understanding with the few
tools in my possession. And I also realized why, from the
very beginning, I felt the need to read each paragraph at least
twice to better make it my own. It was a book by Mila Busoni:
Genere, Sesso, Cultura (Gender, Sex, and Culture, 2000). At
a certain point, I get up and begin to jump for joy, waving
the book and shouting to the people sitting in front of me:
"She quoted me, she quoted me, she quoted me!" In the notes
to page sixty in her book, Mila Busoni spoke of me and next
to my name was that of bell hooks. Mila Busoni knew *my
name*! All at once, the compartment fell silent. I calmed
down and went to sleep. The train almost took me back to
where I had come from, but fortunately, other passengers
who were getting on woke me up. So I gathered myself
together, as good manners dictated. I had reacted like a wild
thing—I like this term, it makes me smile—just as I had
learned in my village where, when you were the bearer of a
message, the others came forward to meet you asking you to
share the news. And then, depending on the circumstances,
everyone danced or wept together.

During this long stopover, lasting more than twenty
years, I have often thought of my journey. A journey, as
all the peoples of the world know, is an important metaphor for life, leading toward death. The idea that my stopover might be a metaphor for death disturbs me. The death
of my intellectual and social growth. Therefore, my
journey-stopover and my writing become the means for

not forgetting, for keeping the memory. Not to go astray and not to succumb.

•••••

For me, it was very emotional to become part of a new village called Rose, in the province of Cosenza. To document, to write in order to not forget is essential for the construction of a memory. Identity is the sum of all these signs and stopovers, which become active memories. They give substance to the present and to the future. They nourish the will and the hope of making it through, in the refusal of having lived in vain.

On April 21, 2000 (I like the idea that this is the date celebrating the foundation of Rome) I reached an important milestone along my journey: I became an Italian citizen and I renounced my Cameroonian citizenship. As soon as I said: "I swear allegiance . . ." my voice broke down from emotion. I was unable to complete such a short statement. I had just turned forty-two. My face drenched in tears, I reached out for a friendly hand to sustain mine and found Rosario Aiello's. Instinctively I turned around to look for my mother's face and I saw Urda Topp's who smiled at me. In these last ten years this couple and their daughter Flavia have been my family. Angela Lozza, my godmother (naturalization witness, mother, sister, mentor) dried her own tears. And many friends gave proof of their affection with their tributes:

- Only the slowness of the Italian bureaucracy delayed the official conferring of Italian citizenship on her. For me, Genny has always been an Italian citizen. (Rosario Aiello)
- To Jenny who is becoming an Italian citizen without renouncing her own cultural identity. (Enzo Arcuri)

- I am waiting for the day in which I shall be honored to be represented by you, a citizen not just by right alone, but also in deed (and in the highest meaning of the word!) (Giuliana Mocchi)
- For us who are used to "patrolling" it was an honor to bear witness at your swearing in. (On behalf of the City Traffic Police Patrol: Tiziana G., Franco M., Pompeo F., Luigi B.)
- To my friend and sister Jenny who knows that in order to change a system, working from within is more efficient. May the strength of her experience, the tireless energy of her actions, the power of her imagination help her leave, on this land of ours, the mark that only great souls can leave. Fondly, (Alessandra Muzzi)

Almost all of my friends were there in Calabria for my swearing in. When I could no longer control my emotions, I felt the support of ten, twenty, fifty, and then more than one hundred fifty people. Only the applause of those present and my clarity of mind allowed me to continue reciting that formula which, I knew, contained my entire story.

Even during my swearing in ceremony, as in all the most important moments of my life, I was intensely aware of what was happening around and inside of me. A friend of mine said to me: "What? You are here to be sworn in as an Italian citizen and you're dressed like that? What are you trying to say?" I was wearing an elegant traditional dress from one of Cameroon's more than two hundred and thirty-two ethnic groups, a dress for grand occasions.

It was difficult for me to recite that oath because it required me to die as a Cameroonian in order to be reborn as an Italian. That morning my cousin had called me from Catania where he was studying and said, "Are you really sure you want to give up your negritude?" Citizen of the world that I am, my blood ran cold thinking that my African side would "die." And the tributes from my Italian friends reminded me of those usually written on the birth of a baby. But is it really necessary to see these two identities in contrast with each other?

While I was being granted my Italian citizenship, I was reminded of the day I was disowned in my own country, and I felt that I was, once again, voluntarily sealing my separation from Cameroon. But that was not at all what I wanted. I wanted to return to "my people," to be fussed over and cared for, I wanted to tell them about my journey. My life since that day; a life that has not been all tears and hardship. I wanted to tell them what it means to be born in one land, to live in another, and maybe even to die there. When I die, my body will remain in my homeland, Italy. I feel a little sad that I cannot be buried in two places at the same time and that— not being able to be a mourner at my own funeral—I will not be able to tell others about it.

I strongly believe in keeping the boundaries of my identity open: the religious, social, and political boundaries. I am not saying anything revolutionary. I am well aware of all these contributions to the construction of my identity. I have control over them, and I try to assign the right value to them all.

●●●●●

I was saying that the discovery of the woman in me does not give me any more solace than the discovery of my "Blackness," my belonging to a socioeconomic and political minority. Nevertheless, I choose to reflect briefly on this subject, because I think that, although the experience of the individual cannot—immediately and convincingly— have scientific validity, it is nevertheless possible to put together the life stories, the many experiences, the various journeys—similar but also different—experienced in a variety of times and space. Through a comparative and non-hierarchical reading of them, there is the very strong probability of discovering that they are crisscrossed by the same constants and the same variables. At that point, the importance of these lives, these experiences, these people and their stories becomes so interesting that they can be capitalized upon by such scientific disciplines as sociology, anthropology, and history.

In this short diary I am interested in seeing, on the one hand, how my memory, history, and identity have been, and continue to be, socially constructed and represented by the others; on the other hand, I want to see my response to how others represent me and how I represent myself. But what is the best way to bring together these two points of view?

It has taken me many years to reach this awareness, years made up of journeys, not only involving crossings, but also brief and longer stopovers. During these stopovers, encounters occur in which asking questions and listening to answers becomes fundamental, both for those who ask and for those who answer. These stopovers, these questions, these answers help to make that "Long Journey" of which Francesco Remotti speaks (1990). A journey at the end of which one should have acquired tools, not only useful for a better knowledge of others, but also of oneself.

It is still challenging for me, when I talk about the "others"—that is, Westerners—to break down their world into men on one hand, women on the other, and me in yet another space. And then there is the "we": we non-EU citizens, we non-EU women, we Africans, we sub-Saharan Africans, we Blacks, we Black women, we Cameroonians, and we Cameroonian women, all the way down to we Bamileke, we Bamileke women, and finally down to me, an immigrant Bamileke woman, who is all of these women in one. The "me" who has formally renounced her citizenship of origin in order to assume Italian citizenship.

The chaos that runs through this type of listing of my various affiliations, and therefore through my multiple identities, if not ordered in some way, can lead to mental chaos and, possibly, to a split personality: a personality disorder, even to madness, putting it bluntly. This is one of the negative aspects that choosing or being forced to "travel" can bring. I feel the need to constantly renegotiate and adjust this series of affiliations and identities.

But the same list, this time "reasoned," "mediated," "non-hierarchical," of these feelings of belonging, has a positive aspect: it is the condition of those who belong to various cultures, who therefore have different memories, invaluable for the construction of a "state of multiculturalism," in which they feel part of a whole, but also free to position themselves in a specific, unambiguous place. In my case, as an Italian Cameroonian ethnologist in the making, I have chosen to be in the "margin" as defined by bell hooks. I made this decision in order to underline the importance of "the authority of experience." Experience that authorizes me to say that my culture is multicultural. A margin that is not a marginality inflicted by those who hold the power to name, to brand, to ethnicize and oppress, but "that marginality one chooses as a site of resistance—as location of radical openness and possibility" (1990, 153).

•••••

Time passes. I reread a paragraph from my PhD thesis. I had titled it "The Anthropological Journey of a Bamileke Migrant" (I had used the Italian form for "male migrant"). But how come? If I am a woman, how could I have spoken about myself using the masculine gender? No, it's not just a matter of linguistic default. I was imbued with the culture of the male, so when talking about myself, I automatically and unconsciously was glorifying only him. I was celebrating the culture of the male. And to think of the effort that my journey cost me! But in my country of origin I had never questioned gender, not even when a rich man's wife came to ask for my hand in marriage so that we would become co-wives of the same husband. I ran away from home not for that reason, but because I got engaged to a white man.

Maybe today, reading it psychologically, I might think that I was defending my freedom of choice. Not that I was aware of it. The women of my ethnic group classified the event as an unheard of scandal. I was disowned. Even the fact that my fiancé wanted to marry only me—and not me along with other wives—made me think differently. Anything about the role or status of women was not an issue, not for me, nor for many women of my ethnicity. Yet I knew and often heard an expression that our men said, even in the presence of Bamileke women: "*Pe ne m'djui ghee ke.* What's the use of a woman?" meaning "A woman is useless." Furthermore, if a young man behaves in a way that can be considered feminine, for example if he lacks courage, both men and women call him *m'ben tto tto*, "man to be burnt."

Amazing what my memory dredges up in revolutionary literature. Even Ernesto Che Guevara did not think differently when faced with Congolese cowards who, in order to free their country from the Belgian colonizers, fired while closing their eyes and plugging their ears. He wrote in his diary:

> I wanted to instill into them everything I really felt,
> to convince them that I really did feel it, but the trans-
> forming effect of translation—my skin color as well,

perhaps—thwarted all my efforts. After one of their
frequent transgressions (they had refused to work—another
of their typical characteristics). I spoke furiously to them
in French; I shouted out the worst things I could find in
my poor vocabulary and, at the height of my rage, I said
that they should have to wear skirts and carry yucca in a
basket (a typical female task), because they were good for
nothing; I preferred to have an army of women than
people of this kind. But while the translator turned
my outburst into Swahili, all the men looked at one
another with disconcerting simplicity and roared with
laughter. (2000, 135–136)

Two birds with one stone. In a few lines a nice, concen-
trated mix of racism and sexism. First of all, in the West,
refusing to work might be called a strike. Whatever it is anyway, it is the woman who pays the price of this racism. Both
ways. If, in fact, in the West being a woman is the worst
thing that can happen, for Africans being a woman is "simply" ridiculous, funny, comical, unthinkable.

However, I never saw my mother, my grandmother, my
female cousins or my aunts do anything that I could perceive
as a form of protest or dissent.

Well, it is from my encounter with white women that the
search for my own roots, my history, my memory, my women
began. I began to turn my gaze on myself. I met some of
these women in person, others I got to know by reading what
they had written. Some names: Barbara Alberti, Donatella
Barazzetti, Mila Busoni, Giovannella Greco, Colette
Guillaumin, bell hooks, Nicole-Claude Mathieu, Giuliana
Mocchi, Anna Maria Rivera, Renate Siebert, Paola Tabet.

So, as I got to know these women and many more along
my journey, I mentally returned to my own people, and I

asked myself: "How is it possible that we allow ourselves to be so insulted by our men? How is this possible?" Yet I would see those same men greet their grandmother, an old woman, with the utmost deference and respect. Then I realized that deference and respect were due only to those old women who had respected the law, that is, had borne babies after having been impregnated and controlled by the males, after having worked in the fields with a hoe and with the baby on their back (Busoni 2000, 3).

I tried to understand what strategies they had adopted to defend themselves from these forms of personal annihilation. I also tried to put myself in the shoes of a Bamileke man. True, not such a difficult exercise, if only yesterday I had been talking about myself by replacing my name with his, by replacing my personal pronoun with his. Let's see: the woman produces children—but in many cultures only sons, not daughters, are considered of value, since females are deemed useless. So, women are valued by men on the basis of the number of healthy sons they produce, just like an entrepreneur with their workers. So, what strategy did these women come up with to prove their worth? They too understood that same principle. In fact, the biggest traders in Cameroon are women, particularly the Bamileke women. They are the most active. They buy goods of all kinds and then sell them to earn money. They run their *tontine*, a kind of private ethnic bank in which they open savings accounts and lend money at a fixed rate. They specialize in dealing with commodities, but they do not question the relationship between themselves and the concept of commodity.

I was talking about the beneficial aspect of multiple belongings because after the raising of my consciousness at each stage of the journey, through all my above listed identities, I became aware and convinced that—to paraphrase bell hooks—there is a need for my voice to be heard, since I can speak about myself better than anyone else. There is a need for *my* voice to be heard. I do not just speak of my suffering. I want to tell you my story, which should not be told by those who I believe may be the "others," or, even worse, my colonizer (who, take note, was not even the winner, since at the beginning of the colonialist era there was no dispute or declared war, which in the end could produce a winner or a loser). I must not be feted by those who think they can tell my story better than me. Malcolm X said, "He [a white friend] may stand with you through thin, but not thick; when the chips are down, you'll find that as fixed in him as his bone structure is his sometimes subconscious conviction that he's better than anybody black. . . . My black brothers and sisters—no one will know who we are . . . until we know who we are! We never will be able to go anywhere until we know where we are!" ([1965] 1992, 30, 161). In my opinion, this means: "I want to be the one to say what I should be called."

Woman of color is not my name. If you really want to call me by a generic name, I am a *Negra* and you are not a woman or man *without color.* I do not want to start an argument. You must not be the one to tell me what I should be called. Do not brand me any further. I am not reclaiming anything. I speak and I act. I insist, my name is Makaping and, as you can see, I do not even dispute my name Geneviève, my colonial name.

Someone protests: "No, I can't address you that way, it has a negative connotation. It makes me think of the slave trade." But who assigned a negative connotation to this word? Certainly not me.

I have to deal with the problem of racism with the world of whites (men and women), that of sexism (white men and Black men), that of tribalism (Bamileke men and women, Africans).

I find it difficult to talk about my gender identity ʋ out calling into question racism, sexism, differentialism, aɪ. so on; not only that racism, sexism, and differentialism of everyday life, but also the neoracism that has spread in cultured circles, in the circles of those who have had the right, and the good fortune, to be literate; of those, like the cultured and the intellectual, who are capable and called upon to decide the destiny of others.

•••••

It's October 21, 2000. I am reading a report by Italy's leading news agency, ANSA. For a Black child "to be adopted by an Italian couple living in a small town, where everyone would point him out as the town's marvel, integration would be very difficult." For this reason, "not once but at least fifty or sixty times a year," the Juvenile Court of Ancona, presided over by Luisanna del Conte, has declared that parents living in a micro-community are suitable for international adoption, but with the limitation of being able to offer affection and a home only to children "of European race." Del Conte is therefore "very surprised" by the formal statement on the part of the president of the Association of Children's Friends, Marco Griffini, who has announced a forthcoming complaint lodged by two parents who have been refused custody of a dark-skinned child by the Court. "We always decide based on the child's chance for integration," replies the magistrate, who ignores what the "case" in question is. And, in her opinion, "being at school alone, the only foreigner among many Italians, is quite different from having, say, an Albanian desk mate or two little Tunisian classmates."

This brief notice from the well-known news agency was sent to me from Rome by my friend and sister Alessandra who

"I needed to vent my indignation with a per-
ld share it. . . . Integration difficulties for a
child in a small town? A child adopted by an
is a foreigner simply because he has dark
ressed, she asked, "If this is the level of intel-
ᴵᵍᵉⁿᶜᵉ and sensitivity of a person in such a position of
authority, what hope is there for ordinary people?"

The ideology of exclusion is the hypocrisy behind words
expressed in Europe today. The term "*extracomunitario*"
barely conceals the ethnocentrism of those who think in
communitarian terms, or, even worse, of those who talk
about globalization. These ideologies, communitarianism
and globalism, are hardly new concepts and actions, by now
they are part of my memory. They are thorns stuck in *our bodies*; it is not enough to remove them. Rather, we must work
unceasingly to ensure that no others get lodged in our skin.
Those in the margin, those in the so-called "developing"
countries, need to convince themselves that they are not inferior. We have undergone a sort of brainwashing: if, for four
centuries, you have been told that you are worth nothing, in
the end you believe it and feel like nothing. It becomes
second nature. Those who feel superior, because they have
greater access to resources, will certainly not provide you
with the tools for personal growth, neither material nor
intellectual.

I am talking about programmed illiteracy, whose primary
victims are women, in the countries of the so-called "Third
World." Illiteracy programmed by the powerful, because if
you know how to write your name and pronounce it, you can
address your ruler in his own language. And if you know
your name, of course you will know his. You become a danger to the powerful man and his power. I see it even today in

"literacy"

Europe: those who hold power, the men, do not miss an opportunity to ridicule feminists and those women who, in the name of a common goal, assert themselves in social contexts, self-representing themselves. Yet women represent more than half of the world's population and do more than two-thirds of the work, even though they earn only 10 percent of the total income.

Women therefore represent a danger in all worlds. Therefore, they are demonized. However, I wonder if it is possible to talk about a panfeminism. In what name should the woman of the "First World" and I take common action against the power of the male, hers and mine, if I already start out at a disadvantage, given the privilege of her whiteness? A privilege of which Western women are not always critically aware. I do not know if this topic has already been debated. Along the way, I have sometimes experienced the encompassing power of the white woman, exactly like the power her male counterpart has over me. If she has one master I have two. If there are experiences that cross over our lives and make us equal, there are others that clearly create differences, sometimes incommensurable due to the absence of awareness and dialogue.

If whiteness of skin represents a privilege, Blacks seek to enjoy this privilege by seeking out a white partner, male or female as the case may be. In recent years, I have closely observed some so-called "mixed couples," in particular those relationships between African men and Italian women. My impression is that many are attracted by the same preconceptions, prejudices, and stereotypes they have of each other, and vice versa. It would be interesting to do a study of such relationships, of the choices these people make. I am afraid, however, that it is not an easy task; the risks that researchers of both sexes run are many. What I mean is that it is not easy to explain the scientific assumptions that drive the researchers, without them being considered racist-differentialists. Having a white wife means access to a better status. It also means accepting from their white partners what they, as Black men, would never have tolerated from Black women. Such as: taking their children to school, taking them to the park, cooking, setting the table, or even worse, doing the wash, hanging it out, and ironing. All the while not changing their mind about the fact that, no matter what, the woman remains inferior. For the white woman to have a Black man is a declaration of war on her community when it is not driven by an instinct to atone for colonial wrongdoings. I realize that if it were a white woman or a white man saying what I have just written, they would immediately be accused of racism. This is one of the downsides of talking about race, that is, there are words that whites can no longer use. Then again, this is precisely due to the fact that historically whites have always spoken for Blacks, something that is becoming increasingly unacceptable.

I conclude. Memories change and so do the identities of the "others." Thus, in the process of identity construction, new strategies of self-defense and self-preservation assume a prominent place. It is amazing that we are still talking about diversity, difference, belonging, and not belonging. Is it so difficult to admit that there are always at least two diversities? Is dialogue so impossible?

There is a very urgent need for what I have been calling for a while now, "listening education." It is not a utopia. My thoughts now turn to those nameless and faceless migrants, men and women called tomato and apple pickers, who live in shacks or under bridges or at the station, some of whom work illegally, some of whom commit crimes, some of whom yearn for a regular residence permit. My thoughts go to so many women. They call them Nigerians even when they are Cameroonian or Congolese; they call them Albanians, Russians, women from the East, not even "*extracomunitarie*," because you cannot place them by the color of their skin, but they too are nameless. In the European Union there are twenty-five million fewer women in employment than men. The globalization and privatization of markets will make women poorer and poorer. Yes, because the bosses are the men of the First World and the men of the Third who are in the service of the First. In Europe, Italy has the highest rate of female unemployment and women's poverty and exclusion is continually on the rise; cultural stereotypes persist. In Japan they have just concluded the summit meeting of the richest countries in the world. They said that they will offer the possibility to the so-called Third World countries to develop through the new economy. No comment.

8

Harassment and More

I cannot find words strong enough to express the idea of the disgust I feel when I describe the vulgarity of the subjects in question.

I remained silent, convinced that one day, from their own "home," I would have spoken to them in their own language. I remained silent, sometimes feeling remorseful for not having reacted as I wanted to and should have. Remorse also because I believe that remaining silent is sometimes a form of prostitution. You are often forced to remain silent, because you are not in a position to speak out. You tolerate it, promising yourself to beat them one day on their home field, to use a soccer term. They bet against you and you remain silent—you bite your tongue. You have to win even if you do not have ownership and control of the language, which is a fundamental element for communication. You are a person uprooted from your homeland and from your language of origin, and you are not well rooted in the land of arrival. No matter what, you are a foreigner. True cultural mediation flows through language mediation.

Being inside the language, knowing the language, often gives you the chance of a quick comeback. Although, of course, I do not mean to turn harassment into a language issue.

At the University

It was my first year in a PhD program. Doctoral students and professors were supposed to meet every Monday. That day I went to Professor A to turn in part of my research. He needed to review it before our meeting the following week. I knocked on the door, walked in, and said hello. It was about 4:30 PM. I had just finished my shift working as a hotel clerk and I was still wearing my uniform: white shirt, jacket, and long blue skirt. I prefer long dresses.

"Come in, come in. Have a seat" (addressing me informally).

I have always been annoyed by those people who insist on using the informal *you* in Italian when addressing those who, conversely, insist on using the formal *you*. I handed him my paper. He complimented me on the work done. The meeting lasted less than five minutes. I thanked him and stood up. He also stood up to walk me to the door. I extended my hand to say goodbye. The outstretched hand can also denote distance. He ignored my hand. With his arm slightly bent, he pointed his index finger toward my right breast. He moved his finger tracing invisible circles until it grazed my breast. He looked at me and smiled with his eyes fixed on my chest. I stepped backward. I repelled his gesture brusquely with my arm. I managed to turn around and escape down the hallway. One of the students from the previous semester noticed that I was unusually distant and cold. She asked me what was wrong. I told her everything. She told me that this was not something new and that this professor had a reputation for harassing young women. I did all I could to inform many of the people I knew about it. I also told other professors whom I thought could reassure me, but who, instead, just limited themselves to listening. Perhaps I myself did not want them to react too forcefully. I was afraid of creating obstacles to the conquest of my great personal and cultural redemption: a PhD.

From then on Professor A snubbed me. In my second year, I went to ask a female colleague of his for help with my research, and she immediately made herself available. She always addressed me with the formal *you*. I had not told her about the harassment, because rumor had it that they were very close friends. He was present when she received me:

"No, no, you can't accept her, how can you, it's too late! You can't burden yourself with this, you can't take on this responsibility." He was saying this to her, in front of me; so much for discretion and confidentiality! He was deciding for her, against me, under the guise of advising her. She said nothing to me. I saved her the embarrassment of an answer.

"All right, Dr. X, thank you anyway. Goodbye," I said.

"She is not Dr. X, she is Professor X," the other professor scolded me. I remained standing. The meeting only lasted a matter of minutes. The few times I had been to see her for advice, she had never refused to help. But, this time she chose him over me.

I decided not to go back to the building where the doctoral program was being conducted. From that moment on I would study alone, without feedback or discussion useful for my academic advancement. That place had become too small for me, and I felt as if I did not belong in the building and everything it represented. From the day Professor A directed his circling finger at my breast, I decided not to be a silei. observer anymore, but to make my voice heard.

•••••

I felt his slobbering lips on the back of my neck. It was as if a snail were crawling along it. Gross. I had been sitting in Dr. O's office across from him. At first, when he stood up, I thought he was going to the bookshelf behind me. Then I jumped to my feet and he seemed unexpectedly surprised by my reaction. It was the second year of my PhD program.

It was another faculty member who had suggested Dr. O's name. I knocked on the door, said hello, and immediately thanked him for agreeing to edit my article. "Thank me for what?" he replied. "Please don't call me professor, call me O; if the actual professors heard you, they might be offended, they care a lot about their titles." I continued to address him as professor. This was our first meeting. Dr. O had begun to read my work carefully, so it seemed to me, and I was taking notes. I was making other corrections directly on my laptop. I was contented, focused and happy. At long last, I was working seriously.

"Professor, go back and sit down!" I yelled at him. "I don't like these promiscuities. Don't ever do it again." He continued to stare at me, puzzled by my reaction. "Professor, can we go on?" I asked. He replied that it was getting late and that we would meet another time. I asked for and got a new appointment. I was no longer afraid of blackmail, whatever form it might take. This time I was ready to give up my doctorate, but not before I had called a press conference and invited everyone I knew, to expose him and his colleagues. I went up to my floor, the seventh, filled with a spirit of

nent rather than revenge. I felt victorious because
I had managed to crush that worm. I recounted the
to a colleague in the department.

n is a hunter. He tried. Come on, don't make such a
big deal out of it!" she told me.

I showed up at the new appointment on time. He pretended to be very busy. I was not in a hurry. I wanted him to
look me straight in the eye. "Professor, good morning, I finished making all those corrections and expanded on some
of the points you had suggested." I was about to open my
laptop.

"Jenny, I better tell you right now, my dream is to get you
into bed," he said it all in one breath. Without missing a beat,
I thanked him and told him to act as if it had already happened. He left the room and I went running to tell everything to a friend of mine, a fervent Catholic, who also works
in the same department. Without hesitating, she promised
to accompany me to the next appointment. And so it happened. When Dr. O saw us and realized that I had spoken
out, he immediately told me he was about to leave. But the
harassment did not end there.

"You look like a nun with those long skirts of yours," he
once said to me, derisively.

"You are the one who should be locked up in a nunnery,"
I replied loudly. He was at a presentation. Everyone turned
to look at him. He managed to disappear into the crowd.
Another time, hearing the compliments paid to me by another
professor, he interjected:

"I can't tell her anything, I can't allow myself to do it. . . ."
At that, in a flash, in an effort to offend him, I replied that
if I really had to sell myself, I would do so to the most powerful bidder. I turned on my heels and left.

non-violent - but responses

Later on, I would bitterly regret what I had said, because, although I wanted to humiliate him, I had given the impression that, in some way, I was for sale. Today I would no longer make that statement. It would have been better to say: if I really have to hang myself, I would want to be the one to choose the rope.

On another occasion, I crossed paths with Dr. O at the entrance to our department. I demonstrated my annoyance by blatantly stepping aside as he went by. Just as I was closing the door I heard him muttering some words. I threw the door open again, and said loudly:

"I didn't catch that!"

"I'm wondering why you're so nervous." Dr. O replied in a very low voice. I think he was afraid somebody might be coming.

"On the contrary, I'm wondering why you worry about my nerves. You don't seem very calm to me," I said, letting the door slam heavily behind me.

Nonetheless, I received my PhD degree on October 15, 1997. It was a personal triumph. Unanimous consensus by the examining committee: "The subject matter of the thesis is certainly original. The methodologies appear correct. The results are interesting and analyzed with participation and with a very promising interdisciplinary approach. In the defense the candidate has demonstrated confidence and mastery of the subject."

"You know, Jenny, they have a bet on who will be the first to get the *negra* into bed," a female colleague told me during a research retreat, trusting in my complicity. I threatened to denounce the professor in charge of the research if even one of his collaborators dared to approach me. She got scared. Nothing happened and I have to assume that she alerted the gamblers.

Then there is that other professor with whom I found myself left alone, who began to brag about how "he can still shoot straight" and, while saying this, scratched his genitals.

•••••

I was writing my thesis, and a professor informed me that he was going to come to my house at one o'clock in the morning to correct it. It was 11:00 PM. I was at my job as a hotel clerk.

•••••

"What do you think? That I've never slept with a Black woman like you?" Professor B, whom I've known for years, told me. I refused to answer.

•••••

The university is the place that gave me the tools to understand the world. I have dedicated my life to teaching and research. That is why it is all the more painful to have been faced so frequently with this abuse and harassment.

The Meaning of the Name

"Your name is not Rossi, you are not Italian, you are not Rossi's daughter."

How many times have I heard these words, when some of my interlocutors criticized "my excessive ambition, my aiming too high." I should not aspire to become a PhD, because you have to have strong connections. My name is Geneviève Makaping. I should not aspire to become a TV reporter, because you have to be Italian and, above all, you have to be very good. These are all euphemisms to say that the highest aspiration for "*extracomunitari*" is to know their place and do the jobs that Italians do not want to do.

It so happened that some people, the ones who were a bit more intelligent and capable of observation, were about to discover my "game," that of beating them on their own home field. I played. Sometimes I think that, out of necessity, I had to choose to use their worst weapon: hypocrisy. Hypocrites are the ones who arrive, pat you on the back and say out loud, "Hi, Jenny," "Hi, beautiful"; they do it, but only in front of other people, to flaunt a nonexistent familiarity. They do it to show their multicultural openness and to demonstrate how much they believe in a "multiracial" society. I wish I never had to write this word, to disagree with its use, because of all the cruelties that humankind continues to perpetrate in the name of "race," "ethnicity," and "tribe." I believe that Juteau-Lee is right—when she refers to the work of Colette Guillaumin—to remind us that:

> Paradoxically, "race" exists and does not exist; although an imaginary formation and an ideological construct, it is real, a brutal and tangible reality. Both "race" and "sex" are empirically effective categories; they are political realities that also enter into legislation. Since they are operative, since they function to exploit and to kill, she suggests that they be kept and not eradicated from our critical vocabulary. To ban these terms can unfortunately serve to hide the relationship which gives birth to them, and it will certainly not bring about the eradication of racism and sexism. In other words, if one could eliminate the notions it would only serve to mask the presence of the social relations of domination which produced them. (1995, 19)

I was talking about hypocritical people, who flaunt friendly attitudes in front of others and then, when you see them and there are no witnesses, are always in a hurry. They are shifty, especially if you mention some thought of yours that is not necessarily considered a problem. Now, however, I go on the attack with the harassers. In public, I embarrass them, they blush or turn pale. Privately, I do not even say good morning to them. But they have a guilty conscience and they greet me. They greet me and spread the word that I am now "protected," they say that I have the necessary, powerful "connections." Some of these hypocrites even kiss me on the cheek, but I dismiss that gesture with the back of my hand. I have also reflected on my behavior toward those people I call hypocrites. In my defense, I thought that even their way of dealing with me was a statement of power by those in the center. I am the one who is in the "margin" and who can—in their opinion—"only ask."

I believe that this exercise of mine is not "pure" field research, of the kind that anthropologists carry out with the suggestive methodology of participant observation. The fact is that part of my life overlaps with my research. There is no real dividing line between my life and my observations. Mine is not always "participant observation" because I often lack distance. It is really about my life. Observation and life go hand in hand. My observation is a form of journalistic reporting. A continuous scoop, very specific. If the classic scoop is based on the rarity and exclusivity of the event that occurs, mine is based on the opposite, namely the frequency of certain facts that leave traces in people's lives. And these are the people I think I will put in their place when the time comes. When? Big question. In the story that I'm going to write. In the story that I am already writing. These last statements sound like revenge and maybe they are in some measure. My hope is that these people and others may one day read what I am writing and recognize themselves. Who knows, maybe they will be afflicted by doubt, which would be a first step toward awareness.

There are many circumstances in which I have felt like I was in the way, not wanted and/or not welcome. Now, when this happens, my gaze is no longer the one I had when I chose silence in order not to give others the satisfaction of making my voice heard. It was a snobbish attitude anyway, beyond the fact that it was an unconscious form of protection.

Sometimes it happened that some of the people I worked with "off the books" would yell at me, for reasons that were not always clear, threatening to fire me. I was on the point of answering "How? I'm not lawfully employed here, I don't have a contract." Many times I chose not to respond; it was not the right time yet, because I could have been forced to leave. And I do not have to or want to leave because I would put myself in the position of no longer observing. I am aware that my being there is a thorn in the side of those who think I do not belong there. It is not my fault if they think I am their problem, their nightmare. Minorities exist, I exist, and I certainly cannot kill myself to please them and so ease *their* pain. I believe too much in life as valuable and miraculous. Although I do not share their point of view, I understand them. They must really be hurting. Nasty business. But how can I help them? An indisputable law dictates that "it is the men who solve problems and not the other way around"— and I am their problem.

Same with some women. Them too. I began to break down the white world into white men and white women when white women told me that certain things that I perceived merely as annoyances and nuisances they called "harassment," "sexual harassment." Other white women, on the other hand, would tell me not to make a big deal out of it, "after all, they just tried, nothing more." How many times have I thought about how interesting it would be to interview them, to ask about harassment, about mobbing. With some I have tried. *Omertà*, the southern Italian code of silence and honor, is still pervasive. We women, ready to despair after a rape and to keep silent when harassed. If reporting a rape is still taboo, so is reporting harassment. Some women say: "If you don't accept his advances, you should not make a fuss about it! Get over it, he only tried!" Solidarity of women? I would like to be able to study it.

9
Daily Experiences

The ideology that interprets the world in ancestral terms and clear
ethnic divisions, which draws rigid boundaries between *us* and the
Other contains within itself a pernicious principle of exclusion,
which can result in the extreme solution of ethnic cleansing. It goes
hand in hand with the rejection of *métissage*, of the exchange
among cultures, of cultural pluralism; and ultimately hides the
rejection of equality and the universality of rights.
—René Gallisot and Annamaria Rivera, *L'imbroglio etnico*

Sometimes you "feel" that *they* experience "disgust" or
discomfort in shaking your hand but, in order not to be
accused of pulling back, they make an effort. They extend
their uncertain and often soft, sticky, sweaty hands to me.
I feel a deep disgust as I shake the tips of those limp fingers
drained of all color, terrified of shaking a hand, my own,
that might bleed color into theirs. For me, it is like shaking
hands with something dying, a mollusk out of its shell,
slimy, disgusting. Gross, very disgusting. If only it were
possible to put it into words. Sometimes these people, given
the circumstances and/or the context, find themselves forced

to kiss you (on the cheek, of course). Then I truly experience the sensation of death. I identify them with death, because I feel their rigidity, the rigidity, in my mind, of a dead limb or organ. I sense the stiffness of their facial muscles. All dead.

However, sometimes I can sense which ones these people are and, if I really have to greet them, if only out of politeness, I hold out my hand, but from a distance. When you are "other than them" it is as if, over time, you develop a kind of radar, you can recognize them and you are never wrong. If, for one reason or another, the encounter goes on, then they start to show their true colors, even the so-called positive ones. And that is how they reveal themselves. Oftentimes, they might not even realize that they are humiliating themselves all on their own.

There is also another kind of reaction. They shake your hand, hard, they crush it, as determined as if they had to surmount a barrier; I believe that for them it is actually a moment of triumph that is transformed into a show of personal strength. I, instead, feel pain. I feel the pain in my hand, caught in a kind of vice. Their moment of triumph is transformed into pain for me. For me, their forced determination is in fact, violence.

I console myself by thinking of those children who, quite simply, hide behind their mothers or fathers, so as not to be forced to give me their hand or, worse, to be touched, because they are so frightened, they are wetting their pants. Sometimes I have fun with it though, resorting to a little violence of my own. After cutting them some slack, when I feel that their time is up or about to expire, I then go after them. I go after them for two reasons, to dispel the commonplace about the bogeyman and because, at times, I enjoy observing those embarrassed parents who seek to justify their children's behavior.

"But, honey, can't you see what a beautiful young lady she is?" "Mama's little boy, the young lady is nice," they claim, in a soothing voice. Or they beg: "Daddy's little girl, say hello to the young lady. Come on, say hello to the young lady. Shake hands with the young lady. Come on, sweetie, show the young lady how good you are."

I stand there not moving an inch to further prolong their embarrassment. The little boy or little girl persists in not wanting to make contact with me and the parent turns to me apologetically: "Miss, I don't understand, her favorite doll is black like you. Miss, you know, they are just children, don't get upset" (using the informal "you").

I would like to tell them that I do not mind at all, but I do not say that because the fun I am having and my "observation" would instantly come to an end.

I prolong my enjoyment with a touch of sadism; I let them go on speaking to see how far their hypocrisy or lack of awareness can go. They are as embarrassed as thieves caught with their hands in the cookie jar. They shamelessly blame their children. They pass the buck. Incredibly, they wash their hands of it. And the poor children cannot even defend themselves.

It may so happen that some particularly "sensitive" children start crying, others cover their eyes, the bravest ones shout, "Noo." Sometimes it happens that, after having scrutinized me and observed me from a distance, the child comes closer (more likely, a girl) and I go along with their exploration. I participate in the sense that I let them look at me more closely, feigning indifference, and then we end up playing together. When this happens, the parent feels triumphant.

Saturday, June 6, 1998. Where do I begin! With racism? Wouldn't you know it? My friend calls me from Rome. She is crying. [Her silent sobs pierce my heart. They have arrested her husband.] She tells me that, at Tam Tam Village, an African cultural association, her husband and two other men were beaten up and taken to jail for resisting a public official. The police also used their guns, shooting in the air. *They* were unarmed.

First, I phone Professor Paola Tabet. She is on the train to Rome, they are about to arrive in Naples, the train is late. I am sorry to disturb her because I know she is tired, but I muster my courage thinking that respect is not only limited to sharing moments of joy. I can neither take hold of nor contain this pain. I have to dilute it. I also phone my friend Barbara Alberti, a writer. I am scandalized. I still cannot understand how this could happen in a "civilized" country. But I have to rethink this, because, paradoxically, my exercise in observing is taking place precisely in one of these civilized Western countries. I tell her that even those who are called savages by "others" have their own civilization. Therefore, we are all civilized. But the Other is beaten and crushed, like a worm. I remind her that in Milan, in that very same period, some newspapers were writing about a crusade against "*extracomunitari.*" I do not understand or maybe I am refusing to understand what I already know. It is "simply" a matter of racism, the most savage form of it, the one that manifests itself through violence. I deduce that in these cases the powerful one is the one who is armed, who is holding the weapon, but who is not in the right. In a context where racist rage becomes explicit, the winners are "right" because they are armed. I do not automatically presume [that the] "margin" and those relegated to it, are always rig[ht. How]ever, they are right in a fundamental sense becau[se, subject] to the will of others, they have been forcibly releg[ated to the] "margin."

I feel humiliated, because I feel myself part of the margin, I am an "*extracomunitaria*." My dignity prevents me from giving into despair. Yet, I cry. The Tam Tam Cultural Association, of which my friend's husband is a member, encountered problems from the very beginning. The other tenants in the building never wanted them, the members of this association, because many of them are *negri* [It is not my skin that is a burden. The burden is the beatings given to those who cannot respond on equal terms; I say this despite having chosen the path of nonviolence. Those punches cause me pain, my conscience does not. And they, those who beat up others, do they have a conscience? White man, white conscience: dirty conscience. I am sorry to make this generalization. But then again, why not, since on the other side, generalizing, they talk about Black people?]

Oh the West,
at least I'm a savage,
a *Negra* who can neither read nor write.
Who are you?
I don't have an awareness of myself, do I?
Do you have one of me?
Don't I exist?
We are not worthy of existing
because the color of our skin
the first, the only and the ultimate identifying element...
    in your opinion is disgusting

But be careful. The "civilization" of racism has progressed.

Remember. Let me fill you in.

The discourse on racism has moved on.

Skin is no longer enough.

It should no longer be enough.

Dear West, you are right.

They come knocking at your doors.

You discover that you are weak.

Frightened.

Were I a saint, I would protect you against this "peaceful
invasion."

A piece of advice?

Open your doors.

●●●●

I reread these reflections of mine the next day. What I wrote
is the result of my violent outburst and of my tears. I
spoke in the language of a grieving person. I lost my cool.
I wonder if I also lost the objectivity and detachment necessary to better observe and evaluate. I do not think so. I felt
hurt, brutally hurt, precisely because I was fully aware.
Wounded, not just out of human solidarity, but also because
I identify with anyone who suffers any form of violence. I
cannot keep quiet about this pain. It would kill me and I do
not want to die. If these "others" beat me, kill me, and
I keep silent, it is like dying twice. So I speak out, I denounce
them, I want to, and I must seek out a linguistic code in
which to express myself, one that "they" can understand.

In the last few days, I have been following matters on
the news that concern "non-EU citizens" in Milan. The
place where they used to meet was shut down (I think they
were mainly citizens from North Africa). My mind goes
back to the local news of years ago:

> People are exasperated, people are sick and tired of living
> in an area that has become an open-air supermarket for
> drugs: syringes left on the playgrounds . . . the continuous
> coming and going of drug dealers, almost all Senegalese.
> (*L'Unità*, March 3, 1993, p. 24)
>
> Here we are in danger of being ghettoized in our
> homes, barricaded in our apartments, while they do as
> they please. (*Corriere della Sera*, August 3, 1992, p. 28)

Without wanting to make a semiological analysis here of
what can be inferred from the media, it is undeniable, however, that there are at least two reasons to feel repulsion,
which in turn allow me to make two generalizations:

1) The Other is always seen and represented as part of an
amorphous and undifferentiated mass: "almost all Senegalese." Indeed, here the editor must have had some doubts
because he added "almost" in front of "all Senegalese." These
"almost all Senegalese" are the same people who, if they were
to be beaten up, would "all" be beaten up, since violence
produces nonrandom dynamics. In this regard Paola Tabet
wrote:

> Acts of violence and violence per se can come from a
> limited number of individuals or groups, but we must
> always remember that even sporadic violence has a
> foundation: there is no volcanic eruption if there is no
> underlying subterranean magma. Behind violence there is
> a long sedimentation of ideas and also of daily behaviors,
> there is a training to indifference, to contempt, to disgust,
> to fear and finally to hatred. History and the present
> bitterly show that, when the terrain is ready, it is not
> difficult to go from sporadic violence to lynchings, to
> pogroms, to mass violence and to massacres. (1998, 8)

2) Finding oneself in the margin does not mean having to respond for the wrongs committed by individual members who are part of the margin. If you take issue with an entire group in order to punish an individual, you are mistreating innocent people. Let me tell you, in all good conscience, that you are shedding innocent blood. At this point I dare to trust that "you" and I understand each other because I have just used a linguistic code that we all know very well; in fact we share a Christian education. At the same time I ask: why shouldn't a Christian, a Muslim, a Jew, or those who belong to other religions understand each other? Don't beatings hurt equally? Is there a people for whom a slap translates into a caress? To "you" who beat up people I say: I speak your language. Might it be that I understand your language better than you do?

When this happens, I feel disgust. Toward whom? That's a very good question. Toward everyone and no one. Toward the system, one might answer. But what is the system and where are the people who make up the system? Do those in charge of information ever wonder if they are truly communicating and what they actually communicate?

One of the rules of journalism dictates that the news be important. But what is the news if everything has already happened and continues to happen throughout time and all over the world? I dare to suggest that, in light of the globalization of the village, the only real news would be to analyze the content of this same news. What I mean to say is that the essential thing is not so much the message as the effects it elicits on the masses. If a message makes people think, it means that communication has taken place.

One of the harmful effects that bad information about the Other ("*extracomunitario*") elicits is that some people, just because they are "*comunitari*" feel entitled to act in a certain way. Not belonging to that particular community becomes a liability and, conversely, provides a reason for the existence of the *comunitario* whose membership should in no way be strengthened by the presence of the *"extracomunitario."* In fact, such a presence cannot make the "Euro-westerner, white, civilized, heir to the best that the world has achieved" (Angioni 1998, 55). On the other hand, common projects enacted not in order to exclude or annihilate the Other can lead to a sense of belonging and/or a peaceful construction of identities, even new ones. Should this be lacking, a "way of conceiving the world and life, of perceiving one's place in the world" that "has as one of its fundamental elements a solid and protean racist conception" would be revealed (56).

Returning to our discussion of the media, what immediately jumps out at me is the fact that reporters rarely seem interested in the point of view of those *"extracomunitari."* This arouses in me an uncharitable feeling, I confess, toward those poor, pitiful natives, whining because they are mistreated by the "dirty, ugly and bad" *extracomunitari* who threaten whites simply because they exist.

What is to be done with these ugly, bad nonhumans? The gas chamber! Come on, what are you thinking? We are in Europe. In a civilized West that has learned its lesson from its recent history. What should we therefore conclude? That all minorities "the color of poverty" and unarmed are destined to be beaten?

If you get beaten, don't scream, don't react, don't try to escape. Do as Christ said—to whom I raise my cry of pain—turn the other cheek. I heard Rigoberta Menchú say that her people had already turned both cheeks and no longer knew which one to turn to receive the slap. There are no extra cheeks to be slapped, then. I want to turn the other cheek because it is an act of great freedom, of divinity, believe me.

But does my slapper know this? Do I have to turn it anyway? It is my choice to do so. However, those who slap me must be aware of this, and it must be a choice on their part, too. I hope my faith endures. It is one of the most painful choices of my life. I would like to know how far I would be willing to sacrifice my life to the whim of an impulsive beater. It takes Faith.

Racism is a curious concept (and fact), dangerous and ugly. If you tell someone they are a racist, they become incensed. It is one of the most disturbing words of our times: everyone fears it and many practice it, but very few declare themselves racist. I truly believe it is one of the few words with an unequivocal meaning. It means only one thing, namely the contempt of humankind, if not—at its most extreme—the desire for the death of one's fellow human beings.

Visible and Invisible

My exercise in observation and description as an apprentice ethnologist of European societies has made me aware of the fact that *I am visible here*, despite belonging to an invisible minority from a sociopolitical point of view. Last night, at about 9:30 PM, it was hot. I decide to go for my daily jog. I put on my quasi-fluorescent yellow running clothes. I leave the house, I start running. After about a hundred yards, about twenty yards from me, an old lady dressed in black who lives quite close to me in the country starts to flee, entering the lane that leads to her house. At the end of her driveway, at a safe distance, she peers down the road. I continue running. On the way back, the lady is back on the road with another old woman. She recognizes me and says in dialect:

"Signorì, nun vaio ricunusciutu. Aio vistu na cosa niura. Miss, I did not realize it was you (formal 'you'). I saw something black . . ."* she apologizes.

We talked about the muggy weather and the fact that our little street is poorly lit and, in any case, dangerous to walk along at night. When I got home, it was about 10:15 PM, my doors and windows were wide open and I decided to do some cleaning. As I mopped the floor a light bulb went off in my mind and I thought about what the lady had said to me. Most of the elderly women here in Calabria dress in mourning all the time, in black. I am amazed that the lady noticed "something black" and was struck by my "Blackness" and not by my running clothes, which were almost fluorescent yellow, with a leopard-print stripe to boot. In short, the most conspicuous outfit you could find around. When I saw the lady running away, I did not think of "a white thing dressed in black." I simply saw an old woman running away and I did not think she was running because of a "black thing," but rather that she was scared because that running "thing" could be anyone, even a thief.

The Power of Words

I stop by Vincenzo Ziccarelli's; we talk about everything, literature, racism. . . . He talks about nature and human instincts. I rebel, I am not recognized as a reasoning being. I tell him that human beings are not all instinct, they are reason, despite possessing the instinct of survival in extreme cases. . . . This conversation is too difficult for me, because it requires a theoretical cultural background that I do not have. He is an aesthete. Vincenzo has a deep knowledge of language and he knows how to use it. He is inside the language, he knows all its traps and subtleties very well. My linguistic expression, on the other hand, is still only a "translation" into Italian of concepts conceived in who knows how many other languages at the same time: French, Pidgin, English and my first language which is Bahuanese from Cameroon, one of the languages of the Grassfields. . . . Will I ever master even one of these languages? If language is one of the fundamental components in identity construction, then is my identity fragmented? Or perhaps, regardless of how many languages I know, I must nevertheless acknowledge that my identity is kaleidoscopic, pieced together like a mosaic, since nothing—not language, nor culture, nor even identity itself—is pure.

There are two children near us, a boy, Andrea, and a girl, Gaia, each about ten years old. The children do everything they can to get our attention. They run, go back and forth. We are sitting outside the restaurant under a pergola, Vincenzo and I. Every so often Rita, his wife, comes to keep us company. Rita speaks very little. Gaia is wearing a beautiful white lace dress, like the ones you see on dolls, and Andrea is wearing a white cotton T-shirt with horizontal blue stripes and knee-length shorts. The two children talk a lot; they are very curious about me and fascinated by me; in fact they look at me, go away and come back.

"Hello, children," I say.

"Hello," they answer in chorus.

I invite them to sit down. Gaia drags a chair over and sits very close to me, Andrea a little further away.

"What is the name of that Madonna over there? She's beautiful," exclaims Andrea, turning to Vincenzo and pointing his finger at a small, illuminated statue placed on a pedestal under the pergola.

"It must be Saint Lucy, I think. The name of this neighborhood is Santa Lucia," answers Vincenzo, who has never been very interested in the spiritual side of people, although he respects all faiths. I talk to them, they are very bright children, they speak correct standard Italian, which makes me suppose that their parents care about their education. The two children had just met there at the restaurant.

I discover that they are up to their eyes in stereotypes about Africa and Africans. They talk to me very freely, I encourage them, I put them at ease. They tell me about banana skirts. Andrea would like to go and see African animals, but safely enclosed and well protected inside an armored off-road vehicle. I do not tell him that I saw my first lion in a circus in France. I had never seen an elephant in my country, although I knew they existed. For Gaia, Africa is just a forest full of huts. To Andrea, I am a princess, with a long skirt, pearl necklaces around my neck and a queen's crown on my head. For Gaia, the African queen is bad and mistreats the children and the poor king. I talk to the children about school and ask if there are any African children in their classes.

"There aren't any, but if there were an African child in my class, I would invite her to my house and let her play with my dolls," comments Gaia.

"I don't know if we know the same games, but that's not a problem, I'll teach her," says Andrea and immediately changes the subject, turns to Vincenzo and, furtively lowering his voice says, "There are two men there inside the restaurant. In my opinion they are two fags."

Vincenzo seems very embarrassed and asks one of those typical questions that in Italy I have often heard children being asked:

"Do you have a girlfriend?"

"Yes, I used to have one, now I have another," he answers confidently.

"I don't want to have a boyfriend because I'm afraid that if I give him a blowjob he will put a knife to my neck," says Gaia, slapping her hands in front of her mouth, almost embarrassed.

Immediately, I change the subject, shutting out her voice with my own, as if to obliterate her words. I had the impression that poor Vincenzo's heart bypass was about to rupture because of the shock; Rita was left open-mouthed. Who knows what television programs these modern children watch, I wonder.

●●●●

Two weeks have gone by since I met those children. Tonight I met with Vincenzo, whom I call *"maestro"* out of a deep sense of respect and admiration. He is a very creative person, a writer and playwright. We had dinner together and I reminded him of the encounter with the children. I asked him what he thought about what the little girl had said. I reminded him of Gaia's words and he replied that he had not heard them. I was stunned:

"What, you didn't hear what that little girl said?"

"No," he answered me.

I reminded him of the details, but he didn't remember hearing those words. Yet he was present, even if he was sitting a little apart. Perhaps I was paying too much attention to what the children were saying, due to the fact that I was continuing my observation exercise. Now, however, I am having doubts, not about the methodology of the observation, but about the report of it that I gave, after the observation. I was sure, and I even noted it down, that Vincenzo and his wife had observed and listened to what I too had heard. So it occurs to me that what is seen and recounted can often be very subjective. How could a statement of that kind, which

I considered very serious, go not only unnoticed, but actu
unheard? Let me explain this better: if, in my account of
facts observed and listened to, I had to cite a "scientific support," I would certainly have cited Vincenzo and his wife as
witnesses. Vincenzo only remembers that the child said she
was afraid of childbirth. I remember that, too, but I did not
give much importance to that statement. I think I was wrong,
therefore, if I left out this detail, putting the emphasis on the
other. In doing so, I was not being objective, that is, I told
the story, yes, but I privileged my view of it. This is another
way in which power is born. If I had had the chance to
divulge what I had heard, I would have put the emphasis on
the little girl's disturbing statement. I am glad I "observed"
myself so closely as to notice this deficiency.

In the University Hallways

1998, Rende, Calabria. "Even if you were to be good enough
to win a university post here, the position would be doubled,"
a professor once told me, meaning that even if I, *Negra*, were
good enough to get a university post, they would create a par-
allel position for an Italian.

Conventional Greetings

I chose my current family doctor back in 1982, on the advice
of a friend of mine, as soon as I received my legal residence
permit. I went to his office in Commenda di Rende. He was
intrigued, I think, because I was his first potential exotic
patient. I was so happy to have my own doctor that, to show
my gratitude, at the moment of saying goodbye, I stretched
out my hand to him, he took it, neither limply, nor shaking
it in a vice, as usually happens to those who shake a Black

hand for the first time or who continually have to overcome their own stumbling blocks. I was so pleased that, after the handshake, I put my right hand over my heart, as Muslims do.

"What does placing your hand over your heart mean?" he asked me.

"It's an expression of deep respect, doctor," I answered. I saw him smile, with pleasure.

Since that meeting, every time I went to see him, which, fortunately, was not often, when we said goodbye, he expected that gesture. The one time I did not offer it, he asked:

"Geneviève, why don't you say goodbye to me as you did the first time you came here, with your hand over your heart? I like that very much."

"All right, doctor, here you go." I said goodbye again with my hand over my heart, but I realized it was not the same anymore. For me that gesture had become only form, devoid of content. I had greeted him that way only because he had asked me to. Every time I went to see him I did it again because I saw that he expected it. I was wrong not to tell him, and I did not know how to broach the topic, because it would have turned into a brief lesson on the philosophy of language. But sooner or later I feel I will have to tell him because it is not right to let these matters slide off my back like a summer rain.

Trains and Stations

Trains and stations are places where I meet people with whom I might never have come into contact. Sometimes we gaze at each other. Other times I feel looked at, but not observed. Sometimes I feel scrutinized. Sometimes I feel invisible. I observe the way others relate to me, to a *Negra*. And I ponder.

●●●●●

Castiglione Cosentino station, 1990s, the day before Christmas Eve. A cousin of mine was arriving from Paris. I arrived quite early. Castiglione is a small station. The station was almost deserted. I saw a tall young man with bleached blond hair, thin lips, and a fixed smile. He looked at me and I challengingly defied his gaze. He stuck out his tongue (a frequent gesture of some Italian males who usually accompany it with a movement of the head, similar to that of a soccer player who is about to give the ball a light header). He pulled out his penis. I thought it had gone well beyond the limit. I let out a yell and pounced on him. I punched and kicked him everywhere. I had taken him by surprise. He was not expecting it. As soon as I gave him the first full slap with my right hand he tried to zip up his pants as best he could. I was yelling insults.

"*Cochon*! Pig!" He was screaming too.

"But you're *ciota*! Crazy!"

I kept pounding away, delivering random blows. He recovered. Taken off guard, he had already had the worst of it. He reacted and found a way first to defend himself, then to give me a few blows. But I had turned into a tiger. I was quick as lightning. He fell. I kept kicking, wildly, screaming, because I was fully aware of the power of yelling to momentarily neutralize an opponent. From the station we had traveled as far as the street, near the bus shelter, where two gentlemen finally pinned me down.

"Miss, take no notice of him, he is crazy," one of them said to me.

I was just in time to see my cousin get off the train. Suddenly, beset by doubt of not having done the "right and proper" thing, I felt a sense of guilt. Aren't there some so-called decent people who behave in the same way? How was this different from the behavior of the professors I mentioned earlier?

●●●●●

Station of Rocca Imperiale (Cosenza), with a girlfriend. 1996. A man, about forty-five years old, in shorts and a T-shirt was looking at me. I held his gaze and the man stuck out his tongue, rolling it around. My friend had finished her phone call and I, pointing my index finger at the man, said out loud:

"That gentleman looked at me and stuck his tongue out, doing this" (and I mimicked the tongue movement).

The man had obviously heard. He was not far away, about ten yards or so. He came toward us saying in a threatening voice

"What did you say?"

The man chased us. We took refuge in the car. I could still see him in the rearview mirror.

●●●●●

I am inside the toilet on the Roma to Paola train. A young guy forces the lock. I rush out and he stands in front of the door with his penis in his hand. He is the same guy I had passed in the corridor. I run away, shocked. I recount the episode to a fellow traveler in my compartment. He does not react. I give up reading the book I had opened.

●●●●●

On the train between Villa S. Giovanni and Paola, July 1998, late at night. I am alone in the compartment. Two young men pass by, they are in their twenties, I think. They walk by again. They enter and sit down, one at my side, the other in front of me.

"Hello, we've met before, don't you remember?" (using the informal you) says one of them.

"No, I really don't think so. . . ."

"What? Don't you work near the Gioia Tauro docks? We have. . . ."

"Look (using the formal you), believe me, there's a misunderstanding."

"So, what do you do for a living?"

"I am a university assistant."

He withdraws his hand from my thigh, as if it had suddenly turned burning hot. They are doing their military service. They tell me how these ten months are wasted time, taken away from their efforts to build a future. I tell them about the Gospel. I take my Bible out of my bag. They come from poor families and live on the outskirts of Reggio Calabria. Before getting off, in Lamezia Terme, they leave me their address: "If ever you need anything. . . ."

●●●●●

November 1998, on the train two women are talking. A young girl, about twelve years old, comes into the compartment and asks for money "for her large family." The first woman: "No, no, go away. We have problems, too, and nobody helps us." The second woman: "Eh, poverty is tough. I know a thing or two about it." The little girl goes away, her head bowed. My mother comments: "She didn't ask us for anything because even she knows that Black people are poor, too."

●●●●●

December 1998. I am about to go to the restroom. A young man in his thirties follows me after I pass by his compartment.

"Hey you, are you married?"

"What?"

"Are you married?"

First of all I would like to know why he is addressing me informally. Now I'll answer his question: "No, I'm not married (I said, enunciating every syllable clearly), I'm forty years old, I'm an anthropologist, I come from Cameroon, I have lived in Italy for eighteen years, I have five brothers and sisters."

"Ah, excuse me, Miss."

•••••

A Black woman gets on at one of the stations on the Pordenone-Verona line. There are many empty seats. She sits in front of me, near the window. She is from Ghana. At another station a lot of people get on the train. I pick up my bag from the empty seat next to me. "No, no, leave it there, you can be sure none of them will come and sit next to us." In fact no one came to sit next to us. Until she arrived at her destination, we formed the "tribe" of "us" (Black Women, immigrants, different people, maybe even prostitutes, "*extra-comunitarie*"), carefully avoided by the "others," almost all of whom were young. This attitude of theirs no longer leaves me indifferent. I am disheartened and I feel angry. I feel anger for those "circumstances" that lead those young people to express their racism so spontaneously. To show disgust, not at my way of thinking, which might well be similar to theirs, but toward my external aspect, which is accidental, pure "chance," as are their own skin, hair, eyes, and so on. . . . I'm sorry about it, but I try to keep the dialogue open all the same because I want, even before understanding, to listen. *They* are my observation "material," all around me, and I am within "this research field." If it were not for the bitterness that sometimes springs from my observations, I would find it amusing that people do not know I am watching them. They act naturally and therefore "cooperate." No one sat next to "us" all the way to our destination.

•••••

My mother and I are on the train to Catania. "Are there two empty seats in here?" I ask a young man. He is standing in front of the door of the compartment. He blocks our way with his arms. I insist. He turns and asks the gentleman stretched out with his feet resting on the seat in front of him:

"What do you think?"

"No problem," the man replies, as he gets up and puts on his shoes.

We sit down.

"Where do you come from?" the man asks me, before telling me his sad story: "I'm on my way back from Albania, my mother very sick, very serious, paralyzed."

The young Italian has already taken down his duffle bag to look for a place elsewhere. In train compartments it often happens that the occupants rush to say that the seats are already taken. I turn a deaf ear and sit down anyway, having made sure, as far as possible, that we are not running any great risks.

Dirty N–

I think it was in 1986. I was with a friend of mine who was also my neighbor, in her car. We were driving back from Cosenza. We were at the three-lane traffic light in the "City 2000" neighborhood. The light was red. We stopped. At the same time, next to my side, a red Fiat 127 pulled up. On board were a man, a woman, and two children in the back seat.

Suddenly the woman turned around and started hitting the older child, who was about seven years old, with both hands. She was hitting him as if she were beating a drum. The man said nothing.

I was beside myself. I opened my door and I was just in time to yell at the lady, "Ma'am, you cannot hit children like that! I'll report you!" In the meantime she had already finished unloading her fury.

"Dirty n–, why don't you go back where you came from?" she yelled back at me.

"Bitch!"

I got back in the car with horns honking all around me. The traffic light turned green. My friend continued straight and the red Fiat 127 turned right. I wanted to chase her. My friend remained silent during the entire three-mile trip home.

It was my first time, the first and last time anyone said "dirty n–" to my face. Since then I have demanded to be called "Negra." Even if I were not to claim my Blackness things would not change, that is, this is the color of my skin. I do not have a problem with it, and it does not bother me. Others, evidently, have "a problem" with the color of my skin. This really seems like a paradox. As far as I'm concerned, the issue might even be amusing, if it were not for the fact that people are killed for having the "wrong" skin color (Tabet 1997).

Many times I have had occasion to ask my interlocutors to call me *Negra* if, in order to identify me, they do not want to know my name or where I come from. I want to be the one to say what I should be called.

•••••

I smile thinking about my building custodian (and many Italians I know). In Africa, I had never heard a person say: "Ah, Geneviève is very clean, she washes herself every day," as she often used to say, and then, turning to me, she would add: "Be careful, you'll catch your death of cold."

"Today I took a bath." "Today I'm washing my hair." "Tomorrow I'm going to take a shower." I noticed how extraordinary hearing this was. It made me wonder, "If they are so clean, why advertise the fact and say that they washed themselves and their hair?" I was convinced that I was, yes, a *Negra*, but dirty I was not. Could the expression "dirty n–," paradoxically, spring from the fact that in Africa, perhaps because of the heat, we wash ourselves a lot, in the morning and in the evening? As if saying that, if we wash ourselves so frequently, we Blacks must obviously be very dirty. Of course, I had no answer, but I pondered, "That's it! They confuse our poverty with dirtiness." I honestly did not make the connection to when Italian children are told their hands were black, meaning they were dirty and needed to be washed.

One time the husband of my building custodian in a fit of rage, said to me in Calabrian dialect, "this . . . *niura*." He did not say the middle word, but paused before *niura*. I did not react. I just looked him straight in the eye, frowning. I have learned that a look, in Calabria, is sometimes more powerful than a thousand spoken words. Two days later the old man came knocking at my door. He was weeping uncontrollably and apologized. He told me that I was like a daughter to him. I did not answer. Since then, he has never looked me in the eye again. I was no longer the one who reminded him of that insult, it was my *niura* skin, alas!

Negra

I am at a conference on FMG (female genital mutilation), and a Franciscan friar is present. He swears that the practice of FMG does not exist in Africa.

"I have been living in Africa for years. I am also a doctor: six years ago, I studied to become a physician to help Africans. I have examined many African women and I have never noticed these things you are talking about. They may have Candida. . . ."

Then he looked at me and at a young Somali woman and added: "Let me first say that Italian women are the most beautiful in the world, but African women, our friends here, have beautiful bodies, beautiful skin, and muscles. . . ."

I opt for silence. I am disconcerted by the bravado and domineering attitude of this man of God. I feel very uncomfortable and perceive the friar's comments as a violation of my person. Fortunately, he is interrupted by one of the speakers.

I intervene instead in the wake of a question posed by a student, who is concerned because any kind of intervention, from the outside, in these serious matters might be seen as interference in the affairs of others. I ask if there is a concrete proposal, on the part of those present, to find a solution to the problem, and not merely to provide information.

End of conference. A young woman comes up to compliment me on the question posed. She complains, however, that "young women of color" do not describe their experience of infibulation and that, instead, during the conference we should have done so. I explain to her why I do not want to be called a "young woman of color," I want to be called a "*Negra*." She gets irritated. "I will not stand here and be lectured to by anybody."

I think she has misunderstood me, taking my words as a provocation. She starts to raise her voice and not even the intervention of one of my colleagues who has witnessed the exchange is enough. I try to reassure her about my reasons and my point of view. The young woman is adamant. "For me you are a young woman of color."

She continues to argue. I am annoyed and leave.

•••••

During the Cultural Anthropology exam, a student, a journalist, talks about discrimination against people of color, talks about this racism that is unacceptable to him. I tell him I prefer to be called a *Negra*.

"I refuse to call you *Negra*. It is a pejorative term," he answers.

I tell him that I understand his point of view and that we are not the ones to have given a negative connotation to the word *Negra*. I am the one asking for it, since I am in a place where freedom of expression is recognized. The student is not convinced; he says he feels uncomfortable saying that word.

"Malcolm X, whom I am sure you have heard of, once said and wrote that no one can tell us who we are until we know who we are," I add.

The discussion goes no further because the professor immediately changes the subject, eliminating our chance to continue. I lost a battle, but the student got the worst of it because he will, perhaps subconsciously, persist in his belief of dominance. I did not expect to convert him to my way of thinking, as much as to arouse his curiosity, or at least some doubts. However, I want to be optimistic: Maybe I did raise a small doubt in his mind?

Listening and Observing

The dominant reason for this exercise in observing could be to detect the small acts of everyday racism in the West, particularly in Italy.

I am not necessarily referring to the Nazi skinheads, nor to those racist gangs who go around shooting or striking the Other with a club to kill or beat them up. Those are acts, as serious and despicable as they are, that belong in the crime section of the daily news. Rather, the point is, to enter the intimate, everyday life of Italians, through their small daily gestures, to focus on and highlight those things of which— even they—are often unaware. It will be as if they were stripped of the protective shield that perhaps they did not even know they possessed. They will be deprived, at the same time, of a weapon and a shield. My field of study and observation is specific. It is not I who chooses the field, it is the field that comes to me, or rather, the field is there and I simply travel across it.

10
The Many Shades of Black

Friendly Fire

I stop by a friend's apartment. I am about to leave when her mother notices my shoes. They are short summer boots with gold lace.

"What beautiful shoes, Jenny, they look good on you,'" exclaims her mother.

Her daughter then says that I am Black, so I can wear them, but that on her feet they would make her look like a prostitute. To defend my Blackness, her mother says: "It's not a question of a flaw, it's a question of race."

My friend and I burst out laughing. The mother looks at us, surprised, and asks what we are laughing about.

"*They* have beautiful bodies," she adds.

"So much for everyone trying to explain that race doesn't exist," I say to my friend, before stepping into the elevator.

●●●●●

"You claim that Naomi Campbell is beautiful because she is Black like you. She is just all made-up," a friend once told me. I had a feeling very close to being sick to my stomach. I was stunned and disgusted by her statement, because she called me a racist. I replied: "You're just jealous, if you persist in saying that Naomi Campbell is ugly."

Whenever we met after that, she often made a point of declaring that the model was beautiful, but only to please me. I could not get her to understand that a person can be beautiful or ugly depending on cultural norms, regardless of skin color.

However, I prefer Alec Wek to Campbell. Even though Campbell is Black, her features correspond perfectly to the beauty standards of the West. But I did not dare say that to my friend.

●●●●●

Summer 2000. I am in the company of a friend. We are at the supermarket. The cashier asks my friend: "Ma'am, is this your new housekeeper?"

My friend replies, enunciating the words carefully: "This is Dr. Geneviève Makaping, she is an Italian citizen, she is a professor at the university. Have you never seen her on television?"

I observed both of them. Silence. Embarrassment. Then I told my friend: "You could have just answered no; you don't have to feel obligated to explain the reason for my being in the world."

She did not answer me, and I did not push it.

●●●●●

"I idealized you a lot . . . don't do certain things . . . and so on," I said to a friend, reproaching her for some of her behavior of a private nature. It was she who had shared this confidential information with me. Mine was an ethical and moral judgment. Later, she came to my house with two

other friends of hers. She was very offended. They impro-
vised a trial. I was the accused. "How could you have said
those words!" said the one who seemed physically the
strongest. I tried to justify myself, stating that, in my opinion, idealizing a person could be taken as an act of love and
that it was not my intention to offend her. "You have to
explain to us why you said you had idealized her," insisted
the leader. Her tone was curt. I did not let myself be
harassed. The "idealized" friend did not reply, but she did
not acknowledge me for many months. The other two,
unbeknownst to her, sought me out and phoned several
times, speaking politely.

•••••

"Jenny, since you have lived in Italy for a long time, you are
now like us. You can marry an Italian," a friend's mother once
said to me. My friend then replied that she too could marry
a Black man if she fell in love with him.

Her mother was scandalized. She looked at me and said:
"What if the children take after her?"

My friend and I burst out laughing.

•••••

Whenever I have worn black, people have commented:
"Jenny, dark colors don't suit you." Once I replied, "But why
is a black dress on me simply called 'dark' but I, on the other
hand, am Black?" I was complimented on my "great sense of
humor." I was not joking.

•••••

I am on a bus to Treviso; I am attending an anti-racist demonstration. There are only two white people on the bus with

us: the driver, who chews gum the whole way, and a woman, Teresina. She is wearing a long skirt with black and white floral patterns and a white shirt.

She is a very sweet looking woman with an unaffected, polite manner. I study her. She is sitting right in front of me. She has short graying hair, parted on one side. I feel sorry for her, because she is sitting alone, talking to no one, and I sense that she is very conscious of this. I can sense that she understands and justifies this exclusion. Teresina is what I would describe as an ally, even though she made us listen to African music for the entire duration of the trip (almost ten hours). No one had asked her to, but she probably thought that we, *being* Africans, would appreciate it. It might have been a good opportunity to hear music from different parts of the world and different genres of music. I had not thought of that, neither had she.

Years later, I actually thought that hers was a "compassionate" or "reparative" attitude, whereby "white" or "non-Black" people take on the guilt of their colonizing ancestors. Had that been the case, it would have been unfair both to herself and to the people she pitied.

●●●●●

I am walking arm in arm with a girlfriend. A police car passes by. She quickly pulls her arm out, only to tuck it back in again after making sure the policemen are gone. Is linking arms always a sign of love?

●●●●●

"Holy crap, Jenny, you're a smart person, it's not like you're from the Congo." This was said to me by a friend who couldn't accept the fact that I did not instantly understand what she was trying to say.

●●●●●

"My daughter came home distraught. She cried so much because the professor gave her 29 out of 30, the same grade as Jenny. Yeah, you know, that student of color."

This was reported to me by a friend, the daughter of the lady who heard this comment. Gossip? That same afternoon at the exam I met the distraught fellow doctoral student and she did not return my greeting.

●●●●●

November 1998. Nonchalantly, my mother and I join the rest of a friend's family already sitting at the table. "You are so slow!" says the friend whose house we are staying in, annoyed at our delay. I think I hit the nail on the head when I asked point-blank: "When you say, 'how slow you are,' are you referring only to me and my mother or to *negri* in general?" Impossible to ignore her blushes.

●●●●●

I take care of a dear friend after a very delicate operation. I still remember how much effort and restraint I had to subject myself to in order to help her with the dressings. She had nasty sores. In order to justify my constant presence at her house, she said to many mutual friends: "Poor Jenny has no one, she does all this because she wants to be friends with me." Too bad that one of these friends thought it best to refer this to me. When she has fully recovered, her boyfriend wants to give me "a nice present," so he says. I refuse, because I understand that friendship has nothing to do with it. My friend has never asked me why I stopped going to her house.

[After many years, this friend and I started talking to each other again. Sometimes she even calls me here in Mantua. She read the first edition of this book, recognized herself in the portrait I drew of her. We talked, and I told her that while I thought of our relationship as one between equals, she had felt compelled to justify why a *negra* was always at her house. This attitude of hers had struck me as unjust.]

I do not think racism is always a conscious act, not all people who express it are bad. There are victims and there are executioners. You cannot put them on the same level, but it must be said that victims and executioners are both affected by an ideology that wants to see people as separate from each other, defining them as inferior and superior or North and South.

Ma'am

March 1999, at a market. We are looking for a dress for me. The salesman, a young man, points at me with his finger and asks the lady I am with, "What's her name?"

"Ma'am," replied my friend Paola Tabet, the anthropologist.

El engaño de las razas

Some readings have had a strong influence on me. For instance, *El engaño de las razas* (1946) by Fernando Ortiz, from which this section takes its title. Other works that have helped me to "see" more clearly are by writers such as Clara

Gallini, Colette Guillaumin, Paola Tabet, and Teun van Dijk. In addition to books, photos used in advertising, cartoons, posters, and tourist brochures also helped me to reflect. Among the photographs, I was particularly struck by the one of a male dancer in a straw skirt dancing on the bank of a river, while tourists in a boat are watching him, probably convinced they are seeing a "typical" performance.

Exotic garments, typical images, the ones that are so good at attracting tourists and of which Clara Gallini speaks:

> The Tower of London and the Queen's guards, the Männekenpiss in Brussels that makes people laugh, the gondola in Venice, the Pyramids with camels, Bali and its dancers, Tokyo among geishas and peach blossom . . . a tourist brochure can also be read as a list of all ethnic stereotypes, at all levels: local, regional, national and even continental—the New World, Black Africa, and so on. In its expectation of travel, the tourist imaginary is built on codified and timeless symbols of hyperreality in dazzling technicolor. You only have to enter a travel agency to become aware, even at first glance, of the enormous quantity of words and images constructed and exhibited for the purposes of mass tourism, which is also nourished by dreams of access to "typically different" worlds, where ethnicity and exoticism come together in a unit that is both captivating for its diversity and reassuring for its own typification. . . . Next to these monuments, inside this nature, just as an integral part of an exotic landscape whose exoticism is accentuated and typified, there will be him, the Good Savage, or her, the Beautiful Native. Ever present, a must. If you want to enter the game of the imagined journey, you will have to meet them. You will not be afraid of them, rest assured. As

bizarre as they may seem to you, they are tame accessories. (1991, 149–150)

I am also an extrovert in the way I dress, I've often heard people say so to me. My flamboyant clothes are accepted; they say, "*they* can permit themselves to dress that way." I have been reflecting on this "unconditional acceptance" that they grant me. Can't my "flamboyant" clothes, mostly of Italian tailoring, be an extension of the straw skirt, the bone in my hair, the nose ring, the banana in my mouth, and maybe even the image of a monkey swinging on a branch of a coconut tree? I must admit that this image amuses me greatly. I see in it not only an improbable reference to reality, but also a great comic vein, typical of cartoons. I feel like laughing. And maybe now I can understand why they say that Africans are like children. I laugh alone. But it remains to be understood which part of us is attracted by this kind of information, of exotic tourism.

It is that part where our prejudices lie, our extreme ethnocentrism—perhaps for a long time dormant or sedated—often a part of us of which we have never been aware. If it were not tourism that invented this kind of prejudiced view of the Other, the persuasive powers of advertising have certainly spread and strengthened it.

How Do You Recognize Natives?

One recognizes them by their canoes, their straw skirts, the tribal signs etched or drawn on their skin, and so on. . . . That is to say that, in order to recognize pyramids, camels and Bedouins are needed, in case it is not obvious that, going to certain places in Egypt, one runs the risk of meeting pyramids or, when in Venice, gondolas.

But what is the deception of the native? Does that dancer mentioned earlier really communicate the "authenticity" of his culture, in that context (the sandy shore, tourists in boats) and with that "medium" (traditional clothes)? In short, what is it that he conveys? And what if the tourist were to become aware and finally learn that, under those clothes, there is no authentic savage, but rather the manager of the bank where, at 10:30 AM, he changed his traveler's checks?

Faced with this discovery, the tourist might become aware of his stupidity, but decide to play along, since nothing is authentic anymore. Everything is contaminated. Or he might become very angry because he has been deceived, drop everything and go home, obviously not satisfied, but at least reimbursed. Or it might happen that the tourist is a very serious person and is convinced of the authenticity of what he has been promised, so he demands that the organizers show him the real savages, that is those big Black men, with the bone for a hair clip, who are in a large courtyard, with a pot on the fire constantly burning . . . I leave the epilogue to you.

The other questions I think we need to think about are the following:

Why talk about racism if the so-called exact sciences (see genetics) deny the existence of "race"? In recent centuries, isn't Western civilization characterized by its scientific progress, thanks to the Enlightenment?

Why are *we* represented this way in the imagination of others?

Why do others see or represent me, if not quite the opposite, but as something very partial and reductive compared to the idea I have of myself?

What have I done in order for others to see or represent
    something very partial and reductive of me, compared to
    what I think of myself? What is the representation I
    construct of myself?
What can I do and how can I succeed in preventing others
    from depriving me of my human wholeness and denying
    my individuality?
What can I do and how can I demolish prejudgmental or
    racist thinking?

These are random thoughts, some of which I have tried to
answer.

The Straw Skirt and the Designer Dress

On a field trip to Treviso in 1998. I am telling a nun traveling with us about an encounter with a young Cameroonian
man from Treviso who boasted that he was known to everyone as the "jacket man." I confided in her about the shame I
felt for him: that was no reason to be proud of.

As if on cue, a man from Sierra Leone passes by.

"What a beautiful tie you have, nice colors," I tell him.

"Turn it over, turn it over," he insists. I turn it over, but I
don't understand.

"Read it," and I read: "Gianni Versace."

"Your shirt is beautiful, too," I provoke him.

"Shirt, pants, underwear, all by Gianni Versace," he
replies.

I believe him and reflect on the fact that he has given up
certain particular clothes (the straw skirt) to put on others.
Sister Teresina, who witnessed the scene, says: "Jenny, I knew
an African priest who wore a clerical collar, to feel full of
grace and charisma. . . ."

The Importance of Marriage

In my language (Bahuanese from Cameroon) there is no word for "race" or "racism." However, my mother once wrote to me, "*Gotam*, the years are passing by. At this point even an old, white man would be fine." I have to assume that, at this point, my mother was willing to "tolerate" a white husband for my well-being, in order to see me married with at least one child. She certainly knows about differentialism.

Black Women Belong to Black Men

During a meeting with some Africans in Rome in 1997 I witnessed an example of "colored" racism, of machismo among Africans.

"Hey, brothers, some of us better marry this beautiful, educated sister before some white guy gets his hands on her."

At the party that followed, I danced and argued with some of them, only to be told, "Hey, sister, you're too much. You have too much of everything. You're the type who wants to be in charge."

Helpers—Gratitude

When I spoke earlier about my changed gaze, I said that I did not hold any great poisonous grudges. Now I think, "Woe to that person who is full of certainty and free from doubt." Fortunately for me, I do have some doubts. Sometimes, more than real doubts, they are thoughts, which turn into questions without answers. But, perhaps, getting answers all the time is not constructive either, as it leaves no room for doubt. Even if rummaging around in my past and in my life, I should find big thorns stuck in my mind and in my person, I think I would try to eventually remove only some of them. But gently, in order not to cause me uncontrollable bleeding. When a tumor is very advanced, an immediate operation can only hasten the death of the patient, who, perhaps, is also against euthanasia.

How is it possible to transfer the experiences of private life into public life, to turn them into science, a subject for research?

Ethnologists used to go—and still go—to poke around in the life, culture, customs, and habits of the Other, mostly only from their own point of view, but with a goal, that of research. My approach was not based on this premise, I simply wanted to experience love, friendship, and knowledge. Now I know that I was not aware of a fundamental principle: I was, and am, however, the Other. The Other for whom even a gesture of solidarity is not free, since it has a social collocation that requires gratitude. That gesture of solidarity, then, is not free because it is hierarchical, and therefore is an expression of power.

"We have given you so much because we loved you." "Come on, don't thank us, you know how to make us love you." "You are good." "Your people are better." I have often heard these comments from some people in whom I confided, or whom I considered friends, as a preface to a gesture of solidarity or before they gave me a gift (the kind they usually consider "very useful" for me).

"I'm not poor like you," a comment that I found insulting.

"I'm not a college graduate like you." "You can't really say that patience is a virtue of yours," they tell me with exasperation when I insist on trying to make my point.

"Instead of buying all those books, why don't you buy pasta? Instead of buying those eyeglasses, why don't you buy two pounds of pasta that is more useful to you?" One day I did a little calculation and discovered that with the money from the glasses I could buy pasta for myself for at least two years. And I did not understand why that should have shocked me. I do not know if the myth of "atavistic hunger" is true. Even if it were, I wish I could do without pasta and eat other things, including books. Doesn't the Bible itself teach us that one does not live by bread alone?

As I have already said, I have made a radical choice: that of not "serving" in any family's home as long as I live in the West. In my plans, living among white people did not include being a maid. When talking about this with a young friend of mine, with whom I am collaborating on intercultural communication and mediation, she did not say to me "Well, sure, you can afford it compared to others like you." She did not even say, "Well, you can never tell, life doesn't always go according to plan." Instead, she replied, "Knowing you, it would end up with your employers bringing coffee to you in bed."

What Kind of Work Can the Other Do?

1993, Arcavacata, (Cosenza). We are at a party. A girl asks me where I work.

"At the Grand Hotel San Michele," I tell her.

And she says, "Are you a cook?" Maybe I should have told her the truth. I probably would have disappointed her.

"Did you really work at the Grand Hotel San Michele? Were you a waitress?" a lady asks me.

"No, ma'am, I was not a waitress."

I expected her to ask: "Then, what did you do?" She did not.

•••••

I was working at the reception of the Grand Hotel San Michele. It was about 10:00 PM. when two customers came in without a reservation. The man was a well-known Italian comedian. As soon as he saw me, quoting from a famous Fascist song, he said, "There are also little Black faces in this place." And I said, "Yes, gentlemen, welcome. Did you have a good trip? This is a beautiful hotel for democrats. Are you arriving from the Italian African colonies, from Abyssinia?" They handed me their check-in IDs and I wished them a good night. In the morning they left without having breakfast. "Sir, when I see you on television I always laugh," I said and then burst out laughing. He neither replied nor tipped me.

•••••

The requirements for working as a hotel clerk were proficiency in at least three languages and the willingness to work even up to sixteen hours a day. This second requirement was not specified in the job ad. Another unwritten requirement, which also applied to other staff members, was also being open to getting paid late. I note, however, that the gardener, an Italian from a nearby village, and the golf instructor and his wife, who were Belgian, were offered lunch and dinner every day. I, on the other hand, ate a lot of salted peanuts, "taken" from the bar, and drank a lot of water in order to have the feeling or illusion of having a full stomach.

I asked to be treated the same way. The woman who owned the hotel was an engineering professor who had also lived in Africa and spoke many languages. To think that at my graduation she had even given me a bracelet. "No, Jenny, an extra plate of pasta would cost me too much," she replied. And I quit right then and there.

I wonder if this injustice was reserved for me because I am a *Negra* or because I was her employee, as a simple exercise in power. But what is racism if not the arbitrary exercise of a privilege?

Christian Brothers and Sisters

With eyes turned toward heaven a fellow Christian prays, "Lord, if my mouth should utter things unpleasant to you, let my lips become as disproportionately large as those of the *negri* who have disproportionately large lips." When I asked him to explain this, he did not hesitate to ask for my forgiveness. I am well aware, brother, that you did not mean to offend me. . . .

•••••

In church, among my fellow Christian brothers and sisters, I occupy an empty pew. The church begins to fill up. I observe discreetly. The section of pews where I am seated is among the last to fill, after my fellow Christian brothers and sisters have made sure there is no room to sit elsewhere. For the Other, the seats are almost always taken or the seats are all empty.

•••••

Excerpts of a conversation with a nun. "I'm a big believer in interculturalism. Colonization has caused tragedies in your countries. Open communication is really needed. I listen to you, you vent and I get rid of my feeling of guilt, of the trouble I caused you."

The White "Cousin"

Catania, 1998. "I'm counting on you, don't make me look bad," said my cousin's Italian girlfriend. Some of my cousins who had arrived on vacation wanted to go bowling. Six Blacks (four adults and two children) and a white woman stand out. The girlfriend is angry, she insists: "children are not allowed in." We know this is not true. I take the initiative and off we go. She trails behind, thus accentuating the distance between her and us. She does not want to play, she sits off on one side. The children seem to be having a great time. Some of the ladies there come spontaneously toward the children: "how cute . . . how sweet . . . how beautiful . . . feel the hair, it's like wire wool . . . what big, sweet eyes," and so on. . . . The children do not understand and ask me what they are saying, they want to know why those ladies rub their hair. Later they will also want to know why "those" ladies have long noses, why they eat *les maccaroni* every day.

Mixed Couples

One day a young man, whose family I was friends with and to whom I gave French and English lessons, said to me: "Jenny, my dad says that you are a good person, but it is better if Blacks marry each other."

Flavia and her husband Mustafà are on the beach in Cetraro. Not far from them there is a family. The lady says: "I would never get involved with a southerner, let alone an African."

Laura is pregnant and enters a store for newborns. The saleswoman is serving her. Shortly afterward Cissoko, her husband, and a friend of theirs arrive. The salesclerk says: "Go away, we don't want to buy anything."

Le Petit Nègre to Teach Goodness

Le Petit Nègre is the name of a piggy bank with the statue of a little Black child kneeling, hands clasped together. Years ago, in order to learn certain biblical teachings, charity in particular, Swiss children had to put coins into this money box. *Le Petit Nègre*, the little statue like the one on music boxes, thanked them by nodding.

A Swiss woman in her fifties told me about this. This was the image of the Other that had stayed with her since she was a child and went to Protestant Sunday school in the afternoon. As a child she would never have expected that the Other would have my face. Moreover, she did not expect that I would have been willing to give up a work contract as a matter of principle, as I had told her I had done. She did not expect that I would prefer to die of hunger rather than be exploited.

Challenges

"What are you going to do now that your fiancé is gone?"

"What are you going to do after graduating?"

"What are you going to do after your PhD?"

"You'd do better to go *back home*, among *your own* people. You will feel better."

"With these degrees, in your country, at the very least, you can become a minister."

Many comments and advice from the Other, said in good or bad faith, have often been perceived by me, consciously or not, as personal challenges.

But Do *Negri* Feel Hot or Cold?

"But you're used to the heat, what are you complaining about?" This is what I often hear in the summer from people who, for whatever reason, take for granted the fact that I, *by nature*, must love the heat and the sea. Snow fascinates me more.

Law Enforcement

"Hey you, you can't come here to work and then you start studying," that's what they tell me at the Office for Foreign Nationals at the police station. I am preparing for my final PhD exam, 1997.

•••••

"Sometimes I hear some of my friends ask me how I can stand the stink of all those *negri*," says a policewoman.

"And what do you reply?"

"If you only knew the stench of my colleagues with whom I have to share an office all day!"

•••••

Carabiniere: "What do you do for a living?"

Aspiring Italian citizen: "For now I am registered at the employment office, I give private lessons in French and English, I give lectures, I am waiting for a contract with the university, I am about to finish my PhD and I have some savings in the bank."

Carabiniere: "I can see that you don't understand. What do you do for a living? Do you receive people in your home?"

Aspiring Italian citizen: "Yes, last year my cousin and his girlfriend came to visit me. My friends rarely come to see me, I spend most of the day at the university. However, if my friends were not to hear from me for a long time, they would come looking for me."

Carabiniere: "Let's get to the point, what do you do for a living? Do you receive people in your home?"

The aspiring Italian citizen repeated the same answers. When she recounted the episode to her friends, many of whom laughed, she cried in despair at having been so harassed. Some of them said to her: "Is it possible that you didn't get the point? We got it from the first line." When she did get the real meaning, she cried . . . because of her ignorance, not because of a moral issue.

•••••

April 1998. I get a phone call from the police, they address me informally: "Hello, Makaping, is that you?"

"Yes, it's me, good morning. Tell me, Sir."

"Do you live with someone?"

"No, I live alone."

"So you don't live with anyone?"

"That's right, I don't live with anyone."

Later, this is how this interrogation was explained to me: "Makaping, I didn't want to know your business, I just wanted to know if I had to write down that you were single, married, or divorced."

During the conversation I always answered using the formal "you."

•••••

Reggio Calabria, at the entrance of the Regional Council Building, January 4, 2001. The president of the Equal Opportunities Commission, another member of the same commission, and I are crossing the threshold of the Regional Council Building. The guard approaches and asks: "Is this one with you?" he says pointing his finger at me.

Filipinos

Catia, from Italy, and I, from Cameroon, are interviewing women of foreign extraction. Surprised, she notices that, when I am present, the Filipino women are very open. They are proud that I am at the university. They tell us about the history of their country. They are very witty. They make fun of Italy: pasta, pasta, pasta. Between us, like old acquaintances. Being *"extracomunitarie"* was our shared status.

●●●●●

A former employer of mine once said to a friend: "Darling, what a pleasure to hear from you again. When you come through Rome, come and see me, even for a cup of coffee and dessert, my *filippino* (used in Italian to mean any *houseboy*, regardless of nationality) is very good. . . . Okay, dear, bye."

Bleach

"How tanned you are. Have you ever tried using bleach?" This is how one of the two ladies walking arm in arm in the lobby of the Grand Hotel delle Terme Luigiane addressed me. I was at the Cultural August in Guardia Piemontese event in 1998. Not to disappoint her, I replied, "Dear Madam, I have done more. I even tried muriatic acid. I have been trying for forty years. Alas, nothing, nothing works." Both women turned ashen, they were terrified. To reassure them, I laughed. They slowly regained their color.

Letter from Angela, Age Ten

Dear Dr. Jenny, Thank you for all your compliments. I'm sorry that you don't have children and that your nephews and nieces are far away. I was struck by the fact that you, whatever your color, love children so much. From the first moment I saw you, I knew you were a sweet, good person. And this helped me understand that people of color also have hearts and feelings just like ours, and all of this has sparked in me a great love for those who seem "different" from us. Thank you from the bottom of my heart for all of this. A big kiss and a hug from Angela.

11

Participant Observation of an Eccentric Subject

A Reflection

These observation exercises that I am carrying out as an "ethnologist" have not been well-received. For me, at this point, it is a challenge, a gamble. The people, the educated ones, to whom I have spoken about my project are very irritated, almost annoyed. Forgive me, but I have to use a strong metaphor to convey how I feel. It is as if I had gone into their bathroom after being constipated for a week and had forgotten to flush the toilet. The truth is, I am not actually challenging any of *them*. The real challenge is to myself: I am challenging myself to recount in the first person the things I have seen, understood, experienced, even painfully, on my own skin. They are little blows, little acts of violence that, all put together, can become a whipping post. Not for me. I am at peace. I am at peace but disheartened. My skin is here with me.

The truth about many victims of the so-called "common beliefs" in some cases has already been buried, under the label of "difference." If someone is a victim they are "different."

But which of the two is the one who is different? The victim or the executioner? I really hope, at this point, to be able to continue this "journey," thanks to having met professor Tabet. The conscious choice of nonviolence can be painful. The only advantage, and it is not a small one, of this choice is that when you get up in the morning, even after a sleepless night, your conscience is clear. I am tormented by injustice, but I have achieved inner peace.

If I had full linguistic mastery . . . which, alas, I do not have, not of Italian, nor of French, not of my Cameroonian Western Bamileke dialect, nor of English—even though they are all languages in which I express myself—not one of them has possessed me nor have I possessed any of them. Believe me, this is not a contradiction.

The reason for my peace of mind can be viewed from various points of view. From my perspective, it is rooted in my deep love for Jesus Christ. . . .

The more I write in this diary, the more questions I ask myself: why should I have to go so far as to defend the color of my skin? Why do some people have to "justify" their status as "*extracomunitari*"? Their *extraneousness*? The fact that they are foreigners? Yet I know very well that the problem is not the color of their skin, which in obvious cases is only the tip of the iceberg.

If my premise was not purely technological research, I wonder then what I am doing, why I am observing. I find the answer in my *eccentric* placement. Choosing to place oneself in a specific position is not always automatic, let alone natural. The fundamental point is that it was the "others," not me, who relegated me to the margin. Subsequently, I chose to remain there in order to have the possibility of making choices. Recognizing myself in the theoretical and pragmatic position of the *eccentric subject* has not been easy. . . . I feared that claiming my "eccentricity" might validate the thoughts of those who believe that I must "necessarily" see things in the following terms: "She can't read them differently because she identifies as the injured party . . . the persecuted party."

Am I prejudiced? Maybe. However, it is important to always leave ourselves a margin of doubt until we achieve certainty. For more than half of my life I have lived in the West and I know its preconceptions, the ones that really take away and deny the individuality of the "others from us." I want to be able to choose, think, and act without preconceptions and, in order to do so, it is necessary to have the tools to "unlearn" them. One must "educate oneself" in order to eliminate prejudice.

Nausea

It was the summer of 1998, we were a group of friends seated around the dinner table. One of them was talking about Italy being "invaded" by "those people." He was referring to the arrival of illegal immigrants. Here are some excerpts from that conversation.

"But we can't feed everyone." "Let them go back to Africa."

"So, do the Albanians, the Turks, the people from Kosovo, the Kurds, have to go back to Africa as well?"

"They are prostituting themselves; the streets of Naples are full of Nigerian women."

"90 percent of Tanzanian men are drug dealers."

"How did you arrive at this percentage?"

"Be careful whom you go around with."

"Besides, when you are a guest, you have to keep your nose clean."

"It's not really possible to always keep your nose clean, if I'm to take you seriously."

"Well, that lady who asked you if you ever tried bleach was trying to be funny, poor thing."

"And I wasn't being serious about having tried muriatic acid, God forbid."

"Some people sleep with Blacks; do you think they might be racist?"

"Yes."

"You know, Jenny, I never thought of you as an *extracomunitaria*."

"Well, it is certainly nothing you should be proud of, take it from me, a non-EU citizen."

I managed to control my disgust. I felt nauseous, not so much because of what they had said, but because I had already heard it all before. It was because these people and I had known each other for years. All of a sudden, I was seeing things more clearly. I felt like I had eaten off the same plate as someone who might—without a moment's hesitation—sell me to slave traders.

In order to reassure his interlocutors about the arrival of migrants on Italian shores, an acquaintance of mine added, "Well, you can't put a limit on desperation, that's why they're coming." I was present and I was stunned that I was, to all intents and purposes, invisible at that moment. I merely observed. Others present silenced him immediately, cursing the arrival of "those people." But what happens in these cases? Do they consider *me* part of *them* too? If so, then would I be the silent part in the center? Perhaps, in such moments my desire to be somewhere else is so strong that I immediately tune out. They were cursing. They even invented jokes:

"Are you cold?"

"Yes."

"Then I'll send you a Kurdish heater."

They were referring to the fact that Kurdish women were setting themselves on fire in protest against the Turkish gov-
ernment and other invaders of their territory.

Many times the arrival of the Other is perceived as an
invasion: "We move from the simulacrum of the invasion,
up to . . . an ongoing invasion. . . . Today, power relationships appear to be reversed: on all sides immigrants surround
the *scant* [italics mine] white community, these 'invasions'
must be countered with aggressive police action . . . the
die-hard undocumented migrants now respond with violence, there are militarily controlled 'Immigrant reception
centers,' deportations, etc." (Gallotti and Maneri 1998, 10).
Inspired by this quote, I tried to reflect on the effect that the
media, in this case television, can have, for instance, on the
scant Italian community at the beginning of the new millennium. If there are 57,460,274 inhabitants in Italy, how
can 5,000 people (let's overestimate) who land here, be "an
invasion"? The ratio would be one invader to every 11,492.0548
inhabitants. How then can 11,000 people feel threatened by
one? Could it be that the West runs the risk of being a victim of its own progress, of its own means of communication
and information? In Italy, the ratio is one television set for
every 3.4 inhabitants; 1.3 inhabitants per radio.

We can hypothesize that, based on these statistics, it is
highly probable that a message—more or less true—spread
by the media is perceived as a "confidential and personal
missive." In other words, every Italian who hears the news,
feels in danger and so there are many who feel threatened.
The message that reaches the ordinary citizen is presented
more or less in these terms: "Eleven thousand unfortunate,
thirsty and hungry people are about to invade just you. . . ."
If the message for the average Italian viewer and listener is
in "danger of invasion," panic, different forms of prejudice,

differentialism, racism, nationalism . . . immediately run rife.

The reasons why people leave their country of origin are many: primarily poverty, wars, and climate change. Economic geography teaches us that when the economic configuration changes, the human scenario is modified from the geographic, human, social, and political point of view; hence the tendency of people from peripheral nations to move toward those in the center.

A Few More Thoughts about My Observations

During my observation exercises, I have come to realize how people who have always considered themselves to be close are actually quite distant. The observation exercise teaches one first of all to listen: as a vantage point, as the position to take. Observation and listening imply a certain "patience." In order to be able to analyze, it is necessary to maintain a certain distance. My observation/listening exercise requires patience and often also a form of "tolerance," a word I hate. "Tolerance" is required because, in some cases, when certain people are deliberately, arrogantly, obstinately defending their racist positions, it is necessary to remain dispassionate to avoid stooping to their level. I make use of that "tolerance" that affords me a margin of reflection, in order to then respond when I find myself facing the "subjects" that I have observed and listened to who, however, persist in reaffirming their racist way of thinking.

There is never even a hint that these subjects might consider abandoning their way of thinking, not even in the far, distant future. Even after acquiring new tools, there seems to be no way for them to change their racist thinking, statements, and actions. They do not even give themselves the chance of redeeming themselves, to use a term dear to Christians. I am speaking of "tolerance" because these people are in no way ready to revise their point of view that they stretch, improbably, to the limit of "relativism": "Hey, this is my opinion," "Everyone is entitled to their own opinion," "Surely I'm free to express my opinion?" some people shout. Sometimes I try to respond, to discuss. Often it comes close to a brawl. Voices are raised. I, feeling strong in my theoretical convictions—in spite of pragmatic experiences vehemently proving the contrary—tenaciously defend my point of view, in other words, that many people (the political, social, and economic margin) are deprived of their freedom of thought, despite it being a fundamental human right. Freedom of thought is a great victory, but that same "freedom" is used to reduce the Other to silence. It is a slow death, a homicide, premeditated in this case since they proclaim their freedom of thought in order to limit, deny and/or annihilate the thoughts of others.

I realize the folly and the danger of racism, which can even invoke the principle of freedom of thought or expression. At this point in my observation, after having listened and reached my conclusions, I would like to be able to adopt a persuasive argument with many people, not so much because I am the repository of truth, but to instill doubt. I am also in a state of confusion, because I realize that the words seem to have lost their effectiveness, despite knowing that the argument against racism—and not only—can be summarized in a simple dictum: "Love your neighbor as yourself." It is not a given that, while sharing the same code, one can communicate, especially when the sender and the recipient do not share the same referent. I am seething with anger and feel helpless, not only in the face of racist actions and thoughts, but also because of the stubbornness and lack of openness that racist people display. I have an immense sense of pity for those who, knowingly or unknowingly, deprive themselves of their freedom to acquire "other" knowledge. They deny themselves the possibility of having the tools to get out of their "cages," cages acquired through conscious choice (think of extreme political parties or movements), handed down by tradition or accepted by the reigning fashion and, later, transformed into dogma.

With this type of person, the meetings go more or less like this: we discuss various topics, from current affairs to politics. When they realize that the Other is more informed (it would be more correct to say more educated)—and it does not take them long to realize it—suddenly the scenario changes. Since they prefer not to say that the Other is a fool—it would be explicitly offensive—maybe supporting their thesis with quotations as the situation may require, they start using the personal pronoun "we." They stop speaking in the first person singular, as if "we" were an axiom that validates what they are saying; as if "I" were a minority (and therefore possibly wrong) and "we" were a majority and therefore right. As Remotti writes referring to Helen Epstein's work: "The 'we' is undoubtedly a source of security: the individual finds in it refuge, 'relief,' protection, because in the 'we' there is not only a sharing of knowledge and values, but 'also trust and understanding'; and how important the 'we' is for the individual is shown by the fact that 'any threat or hint of danger to the group is perceived as a threat to one's own person'" (1990, 218).

On the opposite side there is me, the Other, who continues to use the first person singular and to insist on my point of view. Occasionally, I use the impersonal form, when I try to make them understand that it is no longer just an individual point of view, let alone that of the "we" of the margin, but that many distinguished social science scholars have dedicated their lives to the study of issues concerning Otherness, racism, etc. . . . Not one of the many people—especially those who externalize the most vicious platitudes and expressions of racism—has ever said, "Let's ask for the opinion of the sociologist, the pedagogue, etc." Only on the rare occasion have I heard myself asked, "What does anthropology tell us?" When we talk about a physical or mental illness or the purchase of a new car, we go to the expert; if we want to know the future, many people go to have their cards read and get exorcized.

Reactions to these discussions can be varied, for example:

"To each their own trade." This is said to cut a long story short and end the discussion.

"Take, for example, history books." I have heard myself counterattacked on more than one occasion.

"Everyone writes from their own point of view; look at what the history books say about Hitler: some write that he had millions of people killed, others downplay him." They say this by way of example, to demonstrate "culturalist or scientific relativism." They claim this as if to say "not all things either written or spoken are true," obviously except what they say. I do not even run the risk of compromising my field of research when I explicitly unveil the studies I am pursuing.

Crying in the Rain. 1988

It was raining that day. I asked a young woman to let me share her umbrella. First she looked at me pointedly and then flatly refused. There was only one way to get from the classrooms to the university café. A few moments later, she went off with another student who, like me, had asked her the same thing. I was a recent first-year student. What happened hurt me. Not because she did not want me under her umbrella, but because she looked at me in "that" way. I did not say anything to anyone. I did not even think I could confide in anyone. With whom? At a time when having a visibly "exotic" friend was a problem? This morning I went rummaging through my old diary and found a mention of that day and of that look that had been so deeply painful for me. I had written a poem in English to express what I was feeling, inspired by the song *Help* by Sonny Okosuns (1976):

PLEA FROM THE SOUTH
Who will lend me a hand
so I can smile
and not cry?
I swear on the Bible:
Black does not stain.
Who will answer the plea from my heart
so I can love
and not hate?
I swear on humankind:
Black does not bite.
Who will come towards me
so I can live
and not die?
I can swear on ashes:
Black has no black blood.
Who will please tell them «Love yes, war no?»
And yet again: «War no, love yes.
War is only madness».
Now I am weary.
Oh! Look: they are lending me a hand.
Here I am, on my feet, ready to love.

Meeting at a young people's cooperative, Cosenza 1998. The topic is racism. As usual, clichés abound. Despite my best efforts, the following statements continue to cause me disgust: "I like the Black race," "I like Black girls," "You all have velvety skin," "You all have big black eyes," and more, I presume, just to please me. A young doctor is present and says to me, "I just can't understand all the fuss you're making over the use of the term 'race.' There are machines programmed to ask for the 'race' option." He adds, "Personally, I don't see anything so cruel about the term *race*." The discussion goes on. I tell him that the problem, complex as it is, in my opinion lies not in the set of r-a-c-e phonemes, but in what one thinks it should mean or represent.

At the end of our discussion he tells me, "I want to thank you. If we hadn't had such a heated discussion, I never would have realized how much is hidden behind the words we use. When I called you *a young woman of color* I was convinced I wasn't saying anything wrong. I didn't mean to offend you." Even after this oh-so-sensible response I still struggle to make people understand that my position is not an individualistic one. My fear is not that I will be "personally" offended; instead I struggle to make it clear that I am a part of a whole—I am part of those in the margin.

●●●●●

We are in Senigallia in the Marche region at the Call Africa rally, in 1998. I thought the program was quite interesting, apart from the *typical* music, *typical* cuisine, *typical* dance, and *typical* art, to be offered to those present. On the invitation, an underlined note said, "We welcome the participation in African costume of at least one of your representatives."

The first speech came from a young Senegalese man: "If you know in advance that two million children in Africa will die of starvation in the next ten years, and you even make a point of telling us, why don't you also tell us how to avoid it?"

A Nigerian woman sobs: "Why is there no peace? Why are Africans not joined in solidarity with each other? When I go with my Italian husband to visit his relatives and friends, they ask me where I'm from. I answer that I am from Nigeria. Then the others go: aaah! Or they say words that imply 'Nigerian whore.' But I am not a whore. I can't answer for those prostitutes, let everyone answer for themselves."

A young man from the Ivory Coast: "I never thought I'd see a white man sleeping on the street or in a train station. Why don't you Africans living in Europe tell the truth to your brothers in Africa? I left a secure job, good pay, and a family to come here. At the station there wasn't a single African brother waiting to welcome me."

A man from Zaire: "In Rome, I went to the police headquarters to ask what had happened at Tam Tam Village. An official told me: 'Can't you see that they look like drug dealers?'"

A *Negra* Lecturer

February 1999, three female students at my lectures on Intercultural Communication Theory at the University of Calabria: "Dr. Makaping, I have a friend who avoids going to the beach in the summer because she worries about being asked where she is from; she tans easily."

"A friend of mine is engaged to a man from North Africa and she gets annoyed if he is called by his Arabic name. She has chosen an Italian name for him."

"A friend of mine says she would never sleep with a *negro* because *negri* are different." I asked her if she would sleep with a Swede and she said, "What's that got to do with it?"

●●●●●

March 1999, I am in an elevator at the University of Calabria. "You can see that we have Zulus among our colleagues because the floor is littered with paper," says a female administrator.

●●●●●

I have just finished my lecture titled "The Gaze of the Other: Exercise in 'Decentralization,'" in a refresher course for teachers in Pordenone, a province in the northeast. A good part of the participants seem not to want to leave. The discussion continues:

"Doctor Makaping," a young teacher says, "I really like to travel. I have been to many countries. But, in Morocco, for example, I was very annoyed by the fact that some local people saw me only as 'a tourist full of money ready to buy souvenirs.' I would have liked to have been first considered as a person, it bothered me a lot."

With My Mother

My mother has arrived. Not an event of importance, at least for "others." With her by my side and continuing my exercise of observation I have received confirmation of many things. I have heard, reheard statements that, until the other day, would have caused me a deep sense of disgust and nausea, even pain. This does not mean that, since I "observe" listening, some commonplaces or implicit and/or explicit expressions of racism leave me indifferent. I now have discussions and oftentimes voices are raised. I raise mine too, if I think it is useful to make my words more incisive and to fix them in the soul of my interlocutor. Making your voice heard in some situations is useful because it leaves a mark.

I am talking to a longtime friend. We even introduce ourselves as sisters because of the affection that binds us. In front of my mother, whom she treats lovingly and with respect, she says, "I wish I had a *mammy*, like your mother. Do you remember that *mammy* from *Gone With the Wind*? Oh, I like her very much, yes, she speaks in a very funny way." Innocently, she mimics Hattie McDaniel's broken Italian in the first Italian dubbing: she only used verbs in the infinitive, T sounded like D, and S like Z. A supposedly African accent.

At first, I do not want to believe my ears. It burns me up that my mother is thought of as "*mammy*." I ask her some questions. I tell my friend to describe the *mammy* to me, to tell me what her *mammy* should be like. Here, in brief, is what she said: "The *mammy* is there, always smiling, ready to console and dispense kisses and hugs, given also the fact that she is big and fat; the *mammy* is a kind of second mom, the *mammy* is a *negra*. *Negri* are therefore the only good ones left, compared to the very whites that she can no longer stand, to the reds and yellows" (a word she illustrates by stretching the ends of her eyes with her two middle fingers up toward her temples to better render the "yellowness"). I intervene: "If you really think that, you want a slave." "No, it's not true, I am not a slaveholder, I have deliberately never taken on a woman to clean for me. Is it possible that you don't understand me? We've known each other for almost twenty years." The tone of her voice is very shrill. My friend is very angry. An atmosphere of mutual coldness descends on us. I speak first, "Would you let your mom go and be a *mammy*?" I realize that I have asked an impertinent question, because her mom does not have the basic requirement: being a *negra*.

"You know, *gotam*, there are some people you can get along with, be at peace with only as long as you are the one 'asking' them for something," my mother told me in a grave and serious tone. I was bewildered. I had not been able to express in such a few words the relationship that exists between those who hold the "power" and those on the side-lines. My mother does not understand Italian, but she wanted me to introduce her to my friends. I did not ask her why exactly she said those words. Only now do I discover what a great observer she is.

Usually this kind of discussion, with friends and old acquaintances, goes on for a long time. I don't let up. Then there is always the friend who cuts to the chase to put an end to the discussion: "Come on, there are good people and bad people on all sides, among Blacks as well as among whites." So far no one has ever openly agreed with me and rarely in private. It would be unacceptable for me not to speak my mind, now that I feel free to do so. My job is to be a cultural anthropologist (perhaps it would be better to say "to be myself"), so one of my duties is to demolish racist thinking and make a stand, not only because I am the Other that is being talked about, but also because I work on racism.

My point of view is also meant to be technical in nature. If I kept quiet when I had to speak, I would be lying to myself and to others. The thing that still pains me is the "unques-tionability" of some people's opinions.

●●●●●

"*Gotam*, did you hear that? For them, we're all Africans. Of all the Black people on television they say they are all

Africans. But don't they know that in Africa there is Cameroon, Nigeria, Gabon, Equatorial Guinea?" I pondered this externalization of hers: she had left out the Central African Republic and Chad, two other countries that border our country. She was surprised when I told her that Egypt is also in Africa. "In the Bible it is written that Moses brought out the sons of God to take them to the promised land . . . , the waters split in two . . ." my mother gave me a sermon on the biblical account.

My Mothers

[Rereading this book twenty years later, I realized that I talk about my biological mother a lot, but not enough about my other mothers. Among "my people" they say that a mother is not only the one who gave birth to you. I believe that you can become a mother by choice; on the other hand, I am convinced that I have met some women on my journey who I felt delivered me, but without the labor and the pain. I loved my mother very much; I will never forget her teachings, and I do not want to diminish her role in any way. But there are not only natural mothers. You can also become a mother. And these women are also my mothers.

Edda Guernieri, my first Italian mother. I met her when I arrived in Italy, through her daughter Mara (who later became my sister). Mara was from Mantua. I met her in Calabria with her boyfriend, who later became her husband and who is now a widower.

Edda still asks me every day if I have eaten. Now I live in a home that she gave me. Her granddaughter, Martina Bighellini, calls me aunt; I am her aunt and she is my favorite heir.

Edda Tosi, my neighbor in Goito, who asks me every day how I am, worries about me, and makes sure I am alive.

Urda Topp, *meine kleine Mutter*, who always makes sure I am not too angry at the world because of all the injustices. It was she who gave me food when I was hungry, a roof when I had no home, and made me feel part of a family.

Angela Lozza, my little mother (naturalization witness, mother, sister, mentor), who went to great lengths to get me my Italian citizenship, who wiped away my tears during the swearing in ceremony, reminding me that I was not renouncing my negritude by acquiring another citizenship.

Laura Balbo, my intellectual mother, who taught me how to conduct research and never to forget what lifelong learning, ethno-anthropology, and anthropology of the self mean. I thank her for her theoretical writings, her empowerment and encouragement; without her I would not have known "the elite" of the margin. She provided me with the "tools" to identify the motherhood of my writings.

Paola Tabet who, through her lectures, her theoretical writings, her conversations and her high standards of critical, methodological writing gave me nourishment and spurred me on to become conscious of the gaze of the Other and of my own. The present work was also born in 1998 from an essay developed in close collaboration with her.

Renate Siebert who urged me on in moments of discouragement, made me reflect through her theoretical writings and critiques of my work. Renate included my book in the series she edited, and supported its publication, making it possible for other people to "read" my story and understand my way of thinking.

I was raised on the songs of Miriam Makeba and she made me an activist when I did not even know the words racism and tribalism. When I was fourteen I sang her songs against apartheid in South Africa and celebrated Malcolm X with his words: "Everybody seems to be preaching revolution though no one ever seems to show appreciation to that man over there who brought about a new generation." Forty years later I fulfilled my dream of meeting her. She had come to Catanzaro, in my Calabria. When I saw her I burst into a flood of tears. I knelt in front of her, thanking her for promoting equality among human beings. She looked me in the eye and said, "What's your name? My name is Makeba." "My name is Makaping," I answered.

"I am Ma-ke, you are Ma-ka," she told me. It was as if she renamed me, and from that day on I preferred to be called that, by that name signaling our bond. She parted from me saying, "May I say everything is love?" I am grateful to this mother for teaching me to always look at gestures of love, even when it is difficult to do so.]

My Fathers

[NO! I would be ungrateful if I only acknowledged my "Mothers." I have also been "birthed" by Fathers whom I would like to acknowledge. Men who, for better or worse, made me open my eyes. Men who gave me the opportunity to choose the path that would lead me to realize some of my intimate dreams and my most yearned-for desires such as studying, becoming a journalist, a writer, and a teacher. My first father on European soil after Marcel's death was a man I met in Milan. He was twenty-five years older than me, and we became involved. He was jealous and possessive. He flaunted me. "Black women are the most faithful in the world," he used to say to those who would listen to him. But then if I asked him to introduce me to his friends, he would answer: "What will they think if they see me with a *negra*?"

I followed him to Calabria, but two years after our arrival I found out that he was already married. This father cooked for me and made sure I was always well fed. I was convinced it was a sign of respect, of love and protection toward me. Probably in some ways it was, until the day I decided I wanted to study. He would not listen to my reasoning. He went so far as to tell me, with contempt and defiance, "Go ahead, study, so you can become a poet!" And he added: "Now let's see how you can manage to pay the rent and eat." His words pierced my chest like a knife. But I did not let the pain kill me. My ambition was greater than this sword. I left him without a second thought. I became homeless. But a week later I was working as a receptionist in a five-star hotel.

I stayed with this man longer than I would have liked. What bound me to him? My desire for motherhood? The difficulty of living alone in a new country? It is difficult to describe this Stockholm syndrome of mine. But I only know that when I left him, I recognized the discomfort of dependency and I had a better understanding of who I was, and what I wanted.

My second father, a professional father, is Attilio Sabato, director of the Tele Europa Network Channel. When we could still count the *niuri*, Blacks in Calabria, on the fingers of one hand, he let me join his editorial staff. He did this by going against the tide. I would write, he would tear up what I had written, throw it in the trash, and then ask me to rewrite it. I was involved in the preparation of the news. Then one day, after *yet another* trashing of my work, he called in the cameraman, and we recorded my first editorial. For the first time, I saw him truly satisfied: "More than a journalist, today a columnist was born."

Today, December 21, 2021, I called him to inform him about the documentary *Maka*, the second Italian edition of my book, and its English translation. He affectionately told me: "But you're good, I've always told you that." Then he added, "I am deeply fond of you. Remember me in your prayers." Ending our brief phone call, I assured him that he, too, is in my prayers when, as a tribal woman, I call on the "God of my angelic ancestors" (*ancêtres angélisés*, an expression borrowed from a great African philosopher, Professor Franklin Nyamsi Wa Kamerun, whom I admire greatly and whose friendship I value).

And then there is Rolando Manna, an engineer who chose me to lead his team of Journalists on Metrosat Channel, basing his choice solely on my CV. With that dream team we produced excellent journalism on the road in Calabria. We called things by their name. This earned me a lot of love from the public but also many lawsuits even from the *'ndranghetisti* criminals of the Calabrian mafia.

Even some of the professors I met at the University of Calabria were fathers. Fathers who clumsily pretended to have read what I wrote. Fathers who did not support me after I had rejected their advances, and who, to add insult to injury, called me a "house Negro." Fathers who offered me humiliating working conditions. I can still hear the bang of that fire door that I slammed behind me with all my might, with great satisfaction and pride, barring forever my access to their departments. Hypocritical fathers who would have then congratulated me on my appointment as the first Black director of an Italian daily newspaper, *La Provincia di Cosenza*.

Finally, Professor Simone Brioni. I count him among my "fathers" even though he is younger than me, for his acts, or—better said—for his "deeds." I am grateful to him not only for being the curator of this edition of *Reversing the Gaze: What If the Other Were You?* but for his ability and eagerness to listen to the world around him, including myself. To him, but only to him, have I been able to open "myself up in all my entirety." To him, but only to him (I don't remember if in tears) have I have spoken about the time I was raped by a policeman at the Central African Republic border while I was trying to return to Cameroon. I read desperation and compassion in his eyes. You who will read these lines, now know of it too. Here then, is the reason for his paternity: he made me realize, thanks to our conversations, that you reach an age when secrets can stop being secrets, modesty is lost, and wounds that have no voice and have struggled for a lifetime to emerge, can resurface.]

My Criteria for Observing and Writing

What are my criteria for writing one thing instead of another? When I notice that the things I am "observing" and "listening to," or the things I am interacting with, have a certain frequency in different contexts, I think they need to be recorded.

Earlier, in some of my considerations, I said that usually people in everyday life, when they have doubts and want to clarify their ideas on certain topics or facts, they turn to a specialist for a scientific opinion; they go to an accountant, to a dentist, to a tailor, etc . . . , but they very rarely seek out a social scientist for their opinion (outside of academia).

Once, in the country neighborhood where I went to live, I said that I was an anthropologist. Well, the result was that two days later, a woman in her sixties came to my door early in the morning. She wanted me to interpret "those things that her mother, who had died twenty years before, had told her in a dream." I accepted the live chicken she had brought me. But the doubt remained: was the live chicken a gesture of welcome to a new neighbor or had she confused me with an astrologer or a sorceress?

Sometimes, when I talk to people who are openly prejudiced, they realize that, all things considered, I have "also" studied and that I am not "totally inferior." That is to say that I have a high school diploma, I am "even" a college graduate and, even more surprising, I "also" have a PhD, despite the fact that many people still do not know what that is. This point triggers comments that I still cannot describe very well. What happens is that some people, referring to me, say: ". . . but she is intelligent," ". . . she has even studied," ". . . she has traveled a lot," ". . . she is not that dumb," ". . . her mother has table manners," ". . . oh well, she has good taste," ". . . she is very different from other *extracomunitari*," ". . . she doesn't make you look bad," ". . . I don't consider her an *extracomunitaria*," ". . . she's like us now;" ". . . surprisingly, she dresses well," ". . . ah, but she's bourgeois."

These things are said even in my absence, both by those who want to reveal my "faults" and by those who "take on" my defense. What baffles me is that later my defenders speak candidly about it to me, to make me understand how "we are all the same" or how "we are all God's children." Do they not know what they are saying and doing?

At this stage of my observation and writing I feel very bad. I do not feel drained, quite the contrary. I have many things to say, however, they all seem the same to me, since the concept remains the same. I try not to lose myself. I try to talk about it with my interlocutors. I do not close myself off. I do not want to get discouraged. I fight hard to retain everything I perceive and feel. I try not to put too much emphasis on certain facts which highlight the concept that others have of Otherness. However, I am beginning to feel a certain weariness, even though I have not yet written half of what I want and need to say.

I am very upset that people show a sense of annoyance when I talk to them about my exercise in observation and description. My feeling is that they feel they are under scrutiny. This is not my intention. What I want is for us to try to understand together why certain things are said and done, beyond the famous theories described in books, which few people read or will read. These attitudes almost make me think that the perception of the Other as an "inferior" being can be seen as trifling. But why do they think that they are the "only ones permitted" to behave so badly and cruelly? I do not want to claim the "right" for all people to be racist, but I would like us to come to the common understanding that every action should be determined by a conscious choice.

A further almost insurmountable difficulty that I encounter in the "field," is the fact that many of the people with whom I try to interact, feel "personally" offended by what I say. I try to make them understand that the problem is a collective one, and that I am not pointing a finger at them as individuals. As a result, I feel their collective coldness which can persist for many days.

A few days ago I turned forty-one. I am now aware of being a woman and a *Negra*. I still have not finished reading Colette Guillaumin's book, *L'Idéologie raciste: Genèse et langage actuel* (1972). How many more essays I would have liked to read and how many more people I would have liked to listen to. Reading and listening to others can be invaluable to better understand oneself, to better express oneself, both conceptually and linguistically, or even to behave better. It is necessary to have the same referents as the text we read or the person we listen to in order to understand better, to communicate more perfectly. I am a woman and I am Black. These are my natural points of reference.

It is not at all obvious to fully understand why things happen to us, despite the fact that in the very moment they occur we have the certainty of having been wronged or, worse, of having been wounded in our own person. The wound bleeds even more when we become aware of its cause.

"A little roll in the hay never hurt anyone," he told me. I took this statement as crudeness on his part. But since people say so many vulgar things, I let it be—but I broke up with him. "What a handsome man." "He's a gentleman." "What class!" "Finally, a man who's right for you, Jenny," my friends and acquaintances told me in admiration. He would open the car door for me, at the restaurant he would go ahead of me, pull the chair out for me to be seated. He had a good job as a manager, he was getting divorced, he had been born and raised in Perugia, a traditionally multiethnic and multicultural city, they say. He had traveled all over five continents.

I stand here still hurt, because I do not think I responded to him as I should have. Not out of a spirit of vengeance, it is just that we did not separate on equal terms. He still has the upper hand, because with those words he shifted the blame, and that "blame" has stuck with me. Last night I was thinking about how I could put into words this episode that had been so painful for me. Then, this morning, after I woke up, while I was trying to understand why I had not been able to talk about this moment in my life, I remembered that, before falling asleep, I had silently cried. So the wound was still there. My heart did not ache anymore, but my intellect did, having clearly understood the workings of that "culture" that makes women an object and men the subject.

Media

In order to become a newspaper editor and a television journalist, I had to study a lot and watch numerous broadcasts. This was the only way I could understand what I did not want to broadcast or write about. "The real Africa may be in Africa, but it is also in southern Italy." So said the Honorable Cito of the Southern Action League, in response to a question about their political approach to immigration. He was taking issue with "Italy's humanitarian efforts" and with "the systematic invasion of Italy" on the part of the Albanians.—Rai 1, *Testata Servizi Parlamentari* (Electoral Tribune), the topic is the politics of emigration, June 4, 1999

•••••

"The Japanese with that particular gaze of theirs, you can't understand what their emotions are. . . . Confirming what I was saying earlier . . . the Japanese have that impenetrable expression." This was said by a great Italian female marathon champion, Franca Fiacconi, who was asked to express her opinion regarding her Japanese competitors.—Rai 3, sports program, 10:45 AM, August 29, 1999

•••••

"No Blacks, no Chinese" is the requirement that some fashion houses write on the casting sheet that they send to the agencies that hire models.—Rai 2, May 11, 2000

•••••

"They were dressed like *extracomunitari*." This is how the presenter of a popular program expressed herself.—Rai 1, *Uno Mattina*, December 1998

•••••

How do special correspondents dress? Why do journalists in general who are working in Africa as special correspondents always wear the same style and color—khaki—when it's not

the army green that the colonialists wore? No, I certainly do
not expect them to dress in suits and ties.

•••••

"The people who died last night were two *extracomunitari*.
They were run over by the train. They were probably seeking
shelter."—Rai 2, TG2, February 14, 1999

•••••

Interview by Maria Simonetti with Anna Oxa, an Italian
singer of Albanian descent: "Oil, thongs and extensions."
Question:—So, what is this new end-of-the-millennium
look? Anna Oxa: I would say tribal. A mix of languages that
evokes African worlds, wild and essential. I chose it because
it reflects the many facets of my personality.—*L'Espresso*,
March 18, 1999

•••••

"I'm not going to ask you if your wife fucks a *negro*!" Zuc-
chero responds to the accusation of having plagiarized a song
by Michele Pecora. And the reporter: "What kind of a comparison is that?"—Canale 5, *Striscia la notizia*, June 11, 1999

•••••

"Denzel Washington, a Black actor, but exceptionally
talented."—Rete 4, Mike Bongiorno in *Wheel of Fortune*,
May 2, 2000

•••••

"The fact that Jenny B is a Black girl did not affect
the rankings."—Willy Molco, journalist, felt the need to make
this clarification. By the way, what color is a person

whose parents do not share the same color?—Rai 1, *Sanremo Festival*, 2000

●●●●●

"The Cameroonians are more picturesque: they play as a team. The Italians are trained to play more individually." Chaos and order. Then the commentator mistakes the Cameroonian World Cup anthem for Brazilian samba music.—Rai 1, Telecast of the 1998 World Cup.

●●●●●

Question: "You are on the high seas, you encounter a ship-wrecked *extracomunitario*. What would you do?" The first competitor responds that he would rescue him and then turn him over to the police. The second: "I would do exactly what he said. I would save him, then hand him over to the police." Applause. The third one, embarrassed: "I would save him, I don't know if I would turn him over to the police, I'm not big on the police, I would try to get to know him, to see if he's a good person."—Three competitors in the game show "Cocco di mamma"—Rai 1, August 6, 1998.

●●●●●

Summer 1998. In the press and on TV he became "the Mace-donian." Before arousing suspicion about the use of steroids in the Italian football world, he was Mr. Zeman, the Roma soccer club coach.

●●●●●

"We have no barriers. How can you fence in over 100 miles of coastline?! Meanwhile, these people keep coming. We have to find a way to prevent them from leaving Albania." This is how a high-ranking prelate answers the question:

"How do we solve the immigration problem?"—Tg 3,
August 5, 1998.

•••••

Reggio Calabria, January 4, 2001. I am invited to participate
in a television program organized by a local TV station, the
Commission on Equal Opportunities. Just as expected and
on cue, racism is mentioned. I had been told that the topic
was multiculturalism. We are talking before recording the
broadcast. I get the feeling that the expectation is to say only
good things about Calabria. I do not agree. Dr. Y, like me,
a guest on the program, angrily turns to me: "Far be it from
me to offend Dr. Makaping."

I replied decisively: "Doctor, I don't understand why I
should be touchy if racism is mentioned. I am doing research
on these phenomena. You can express your ideas, without
worrying about my susceptibility. We are both intellectuals."

•••••

"To tell the truth, this thing that white people invented is
not a good thing. What? You suck another person's mouth
and you don't know if their mouth stinks, if their teeth are
okay, no, it's not a good thing." That's what my mother told
me. She spends whole days in front of the television. "These
white people do it all day, from morning till night. If someone did that to me, I would feel like throwing up." I was careful not to tell her that I knew exactly what practice she was
talking about.

My Gaze

I consider the unconscious ignorance of that young college
graduate who comes into the office and from another room

shouts, "Work, slave!" She keeps at a safe distance so as not to get a response. From the room next door I echo her, "Work, slave!" Silence. Another coworker and I had worked the entire night to meet the deadline for an assignment.

I look with sorrow at the feeling of hatred of that man and woman who, in conversation, want to make sure I am paying attention: "Gypsies are all thieves." "They should go back to their own country." "They're called Romany, they're Italian, they've been living here for hundreds of years and they're not all thieves," I reply. Dead silence.

I look without anger, but forcefully, at that coworker who taunts me with "ablabla, bleleble, blablele," at my difficulty in reading the Italian language.

I look at that brilliant young man who says to me, "Jenny, today I met some of your countrymen," and adds, "they're all from Senegal." Yet he knows very well that I am from Cameroon. Why is Africa still considered one country?

I stare in astonishment at that CEO who tells his employees, rendered powerless by the fear of losing their jobs: "we're not firing anyone here, but we're putting you in a position to leave"; "if I don't like you, the owners won't like you either"; "you're all here because I want you to be." With pen and paper I write this down.

I look at myself looking at others, I question myself and I worry. I consider the problem of observation. Am I a participant simply because I am present while things are happening and everyone, or almost everyone, knows that I am an anthropologist? Do my observations and notes have, as their only purpose, the telling of the stories, even if this is scientific? How should I react to these events? Should I intervene or not? If I intervene, do I in some way obstruct the course of events? One can intervene not only with words, but also with one's gaze. During the observation, can the researcher totally set aside her own subjectivity, her own point of view, her own culture, her own convictions? Or does she also have to constantly remind herself—and therefore intervene—that the purpose of her work is also educational?

I am an observer who often chooses to be an interventionist. It's hard, because it involves lecturing. In such cases, some respond, "We don't take lessons from anyone." A certain noninterventionist remark can border on cynicism. What to do in the face of that "primitive" who, on the basis of his age-old culture, immolates a virgin on the altar of his gods for the prosperity of the tribe? What to do when confronting that already prosperous nation that thinks that the electric chair, the firing squad, hanging, the lethal injection are the best solutions for protecting its society from criminals?

We in the margin express ourselves. From my margin I take a position, knowing fully well that mine, like theirs after all, is not the only truth. I am, however, ready to mediate, to discuss, but I am convinced that first we must have a very solid shared belief: life in and of itself is valuable.

Private Diary

Listening is not only an expression of respect, a show of good manners. Listening is strategic, it is observation. It is the principle of analysis that can also lead to drawing of some conclusions. This may be the summary of a year's observation of the various "others" who, from time to time, I met along the way, often by chance. I did not seek out a specific field of research, I was already inside the field. It was the field that came to me.

I am afraid that as time goes by, with all these observations of others and of myself, I run the risk of becoming the specialist of my "Blackness" and "Otherness." It is a bit as if, through all my lectures around Italy, through the meetings with young people and with the less than young, I spent all my time explaining to people my reason for being in the world. Ah! How less tedious and tiring it would have been to justify not only who I am, but why I too exist. This thought immediately occurred to me and I wrote it down. I hope later on to be able to decipher its deeper meanings.

When will I stop identifying as a woman "of color," a *Negra* (as I want to be called) and become a person in general, a woman, or Geneviève Makaping in particular? Whose problem is it? Theirs or mine? What I mean is that my effort, at times bordering on discomfort, is to make my own a problem, a concern that often does not belong to me. This statement is curious because it denotes a certain mistrust on my part in observing the behavior of others toward me and toward those who, like me, are in the margin.

What should I do? In the name of scientific research in the field, should I maintain perfect composure, complete coolness, and continue as if I were "other than me"? Yet I am the interested party, the passive object of their social constructs and, at the same time, the subject, in as much as I am a researcher who wants to understand what processes lead "others" to the creation of their mental and social constructs. Can I emotionally be distant from this?

During the meetings I had with others, I often caught myself thinking that it is amazing, almost impossible to believe, that we are still here talking about diversity, about belonging and not belonging. I was struggling with the fact that when we talked about diversity and Otherness, I was always the Other, the different one. I have always strived to make people understand that there are at least two differences, almost always in vain.

In any case, there was a lively interest in the discussion on the part of the audience in front of me, interested in my diversity, often forgetting their own. The pulse of the public beat very strongly, but, paradoxically, interest waned when I then sought confrontation with a single person. This is also something I want to probe. It might be interesting to understand why, in a group, people are comfortable confronting each other, while as individuals, less so. Maybe the group does not have a face, so it does not risk losing face? I try to continue the dialogue in private, because for some time now I have been convinced that there is an urgent need for "listening education," even before listening itself. Then we have to move on to problematization, that is, to discussion (confrontation/mediation) in order to identify one or more hypotheses of solution.

One of the fundamental rules for my work is to maintain a 360-degree range of observation. A superficial observation is risky, it can frustrate my effort to "explain" why I am Other. Looking for and catching hold of the "deep signals" in the subjects I observe becomes important for my growth. You can look for the mote in the other person's eye, but you must be careful that it does not become a beam in your own. In short, having to continually redefine and explain my belonging on the one hand and, on the other, having to look for the reasons for my exclusion, can make me ignore the fact that the others in front of me, or at least some of them, want to and are trying to redefine their own identity through the dialectical relationship with me. This calls for continuous mediation.

Differentialist and Integrated: My Conflicts

I have spoken of the difficulty of giving form a content. This difficulty is not due to a lack of intelligence but to a lack of tools for expression and translation. For me, a Bamileke woman, it is not at all easy to consistently translate the concepts I have formulated and elaborated in my own language in a satisfactory way. Even if I were to succeed, somehow their impact would be lost. So, studying has been a saving grace for me. First the diploma, then the degree, and finally the PhD. While among my own people each of these events was greeted with festivities and blessings, here in the West I was constantly reminded of my advanced age for these achievements or, even worse, I was told that now, with all these diplomas, at the very least I could become a cabinet minister in my country.

The more witty ones asked me: "What are you going to do when you grow up?" or sent me greeting cards: "You have to run hard if you want to be first. What race do you want to be in?" But the question is always the same: "So now, what are you going to do?" I have no trouble believing in the good faith of those who express themselves in these terms, but therein lies the trouble. My goals are important, not because of the diplomas in and of themselves, but because of their symbolic weight. I do not want to say "*zi bwana, yessa massa*" or "*zi, badrone*," especially to those who are in the wrong.

"Daughter, you have finished paying your debt to the country of the whites," my mother told me. She also repeated this to me this winter, the first of the new millennium. My fever had spiked to 103. I did not understand what she meant. After I had completely recovered, those words were still rattling around in my brain. I asked for enlightenment. "We'll talk tonight," she replied. In the evening, she wanted to be the one to light the fireplace, arranging the wood as we do in the village. She seasoned the chicken with spices brought from home. As she roasted it, I listened: "*Gotam*, we always know where we are born, we can, as far as

possible, know where we'll be reborn and where w[e]
You chose the country of the whites. Now you a[re]
white person, you have new rights, your crede[ntials]
acceptable. In this place, you can have a husband, a home, a
job, and children. But never forget where you come from,
especially never, never forget—do you understand?—that
you are the King's daughter." I jumped at the chance,
given the moment, to remind her of an old statement of
hers: "*Mmà*, once in one of your letters you told me that the
years are passing and that even an old white man would do
for me as a husband, what have you got against whites?"
Looking at me severely, she called me by name (despite the
fact that I became her husband when my father died):
"Makaping, open your ears wide. An old man is a Man, he
can make children."

Once I got rid of the doubt that in her letter my mother
had not merely spoken to me of differences in terms of color,
Black/white, but rather of belonging, the theoretical question of identity conflict has never left me. She spoke of the
old white man because I am now a "white" woman and therefore, as such a woman I would have a better chance. In my
country not even an old Black man would take me for a wife
because, at forty, I am almost no longer a woman. I could no
longer guarantee him wealth: children. Among "my people,"
when a barren woman dies she is buried with a stone in her
hand.

My conflicts with the Western world are not only external, physical, but also psychological, almost spiritual. Often
I feel torn apart by contradictory feelings and thoughts: to
do as "they" do and be understood, accepted and tolerated
by "them," at the cost of betraying my "tribal" principles, the
repository of my spirit? I come from a large family where,
along with respect for older people, I was instilled with the

principle of dignity. In my language the word "shame" is heavily loaded and used in an active way. In fact, if an older person questions you, "*Seu tche kuuaa?* Doesn't shame invade you?" (I am aware that this is a loose translation), you should feel infinitely humiliated because you are guilty.

When, for the umpteenth time, a professor yelled at me, "Go away, you're fired, get out of here!" I, in the same tone, replied, "Of course I'm going away, I'm not under doctor's orders to stay here." Other times I never answered, but I never lowered my head in submission. I had nothing to lose, I was not legally employed. Intimidation, in fact, does not necessarily reside within a formal relationship, such as that between employer and employee, it is also a cultural expression of power.

During a seminar at the Department of Sociology at the University of Calabria, a student asked me, "What strategies have you adopted to defend yourself from Western imperialism?" To be frank, when I came to the West, if on the one hand I had never had any illusions that anything would be granted to me for free, on the other hand I had never assumed that I would have to use strategies. So, in the West, the very principle of dignity that I mentioned before has characterized my borderline relationship with them. Many times I thought that, if I maintained my dignity, they would have to feel overcome with shame.

Eccentricity became my strategy, the place from which to send out my voice. I am eccentric. I belong to a center that is not theirs. And they find me quirky. I also feel privileged, compared to those like me, since I can speak, not accept, I can say no, not nod; I am the center of those like me, and all together then we are the margin. I am a synecdoche, the part for the whole, the singular for the plural. Am I being presumptuous?

Today talking about multiculturalism is very fashionable, as is talking about interculturalism. In my opinion, cultural integration should mean the dynamic acquisition of other people's cultural data, while remaining intact. It cannot be assimilation, which implies the dissolution of one's own cultural data.

I have almost reached the end of my not-so-intimate diary. A thought crosses my mind that at times makes me feel anguished. If I were to spend my life in academia, continuing to talk about Otherness, I would run the risk of spending my life explaining to others why I am Black, that is, why the color of my skin is black. The point, and I suppress a smile, is that I do not know why the pigmentation of my skin is the way it is, despite knowing exactly why I became Black.

Acknowledgments

I am thankful to Caterina Romeo who was the first to believe in a translation of *Reversing the Gaze: What If the Other Were You?* and to propose it as the inaugural text of the Other Voices of Italy series. Moreover, Caterina offered insightful advice and suggestions to improve this manuscript. Without her initiative, this translation would not have been possible.

I am also grateful for the competence and passion with which Giovanna Bellesia Contuzzi and Victoria Offredi Poletto translated the text. I am deeply appreciative of them for respecting my voice and for finding sensitive solutions to difficult translation choices.

Lastly, I would like to express my gratitude to Eilis Kierans, Alessandro Vettori, and Sandra Waters, who warmly welcomed *Reversing the Gaze* into this inspiring book series. I could not be happier than to see my text released in a series that aims to bring a discourse produced in the margin to the center of a linguistic and cultural power system.

Glossary

Differentialism is used as a pejorative form of the term "difference." Differences exist, but it is not acceptable to make a doctrine of the exclusion of the Other starting essentially from a series of differences, whatever they are.

Eccentric is an adjective that, according to the dictionary, can mean both not placed centrally as well as unconventional and slightly strange. Both meanings of this term are used in this text.

Extracomunitari literally indicates people with non-EU passports who entered a country within the European Union. It was used through the 1990s and the 2000s, and its use in Italian seems to have decreased in the past decade. It was often perceived as referring to people from outside "our" community

Golum is Makaping's rank, in the hierarchy of the nobility of Bamileke people, literally it means "the woman who lives in the house next door to the king's." *Go* means noblewoman. *Tam* means house adjacent to that of the king (*Gne*). Makaping's mother is *Go-Gne*. Her father was not a nobleman. At the time, it was an unprecedented scandal that her mother eloped with a commoner. Makaping's mother was able to do so because she was no longer in the village, but in the city, with Père Takala.

Negra is the Italian feminine singular which Makaping uses to define herself. Racial terms have different connotations in Italian and English and the stories of oppression that are

171

associated with this term in both languages need to be explored by emphasizing similarities and equally illuminating differences (Scacchi 2012)—a task that goes well beyond this volume.

To put it bluntly, the term *negra*, which starts with a lowercase initial, cannot be literally translated into English, since it has three possible translations. First, *negra* could be translated as "Black." Indeed, the term comes from the word which in Latin means black. The literal translation of Black in Italian is *nera*. It should be noted that in many Italian dialects there is no difference between the two terms, and dialects influence the ways in which Italian is spoken. The term *niura* in Calabrian dialect, which occurs in this volume, is an example of this use.

Second, the Italian term with a lowercase initial could also be translated in English as "Negro." However, a quick search on Google Ngram shows that the term is used much less frequently than it was before the late 1960s and it is often perceived as "socially unacceptable" in English (Palmer 2010, n.p.).

A third possible translation of the meaning of the term in English could be the n-word. The term not only describes a physical feature, but also connotes a group of people through a specific bodily feature—their skin color—which implies by those who use it a judgment of physical, intellectual, and moral inferiority. Indeed, this term is an insult in today's Italy when used in combination with a disparaging adjective or pronounced in a particular tone of voice (Faloppa 2011, 21).

However, the term starting with a lowercase initial in its different meanings cannot capture the connotation of the term *Negra* as Makaping employs it in the original Italian text. Capitonyms are rarely used in Italian, and Makaping's use adheres to W. E. B. Du Bois's request to use the capitonyms to indicate a social group made of individuals who share common experiences. According to Du Bois, "Eight million Americans are entitled to a capital letter" (1899, 1). For the same reason, we have capitalized the adjective "Black" (Coleman 2020).

The decision to leave the *Negra* and *negro* untranslated aims to show *in* and *through* language that the Black experience is heterogeneous and that racism does not take the same shapes and form everywhere in the world (Hall 1990). It is important to note that the deconstruction of derogatory terms in this book was inspired not exclusively by reflections about race and racism in the United States. The term *Negra* and the reference to Makaping's Blackness was stirred by the *négritude* movement, and Aimé Césaire's, Léon-Gontran Damas's, and Léopold Sédar Senghor's work.

The Other (capitalized) is a noun that, according to the Merriam-Webster dictionary, indicates "one considered by members of a dominant group as alien, exotic, threatening, or inferior (as because of different racial, sexual, or cultural characteristics)."

Tradition in this text is meant as an impediment to understanding cultural diversity. As Ugo Fabietti writes:

Faced with the problem of correctly understanding what ethnicity, ethnic identity, ethnicity or the ethnic border and frontier are, we have to start a small Copernican revolution. That is, we must adopt an intellectual attitude that consists in not taking for granted those ideas that the strength of tradition has imposed on us as if they were "obvious." This attitude is called "suspension of judgment" and should correspond to what happens when we observe from the point of view of anthropology. It is not easy to assume this viewpoint, since tradition, that is, the habit of thinking in a certain way that has been rooted in our language and in our representations, has imprisoned us in powerful chains. (1995, 11–12)

References

Adichie, Chimamanda Ngozi. 2009. "The Danger of a Single Story." TED video. https://www.ted.com/talks/chimamanda _ngozi_adichie_the_danger_of_a_single_story.

Angioni, Giulio. 1998. "Razzismo mite?" In *Io non sono razzista ma . . . Strumenti per disimparare il razzismo*, edited by Paola Tabet and Silvana Di Bella, 54–59. Rome: Anicia.

Balbo, Laura. 2001. "Presentazione." In *Traiettorie di sguardi. E se gli altri foste voi?*, by Geneviève Makaping, v–vi. Soveria Mannelli: Rubbettino.

Benchouiha, Lucie. 2006. "Hybrid Identities? Immigrant Women's Writing in Italy." *Italian Studies* 61 (2): 251–262.

Bhabha, Homi K. 1994. "Of Mimicry and Man." In *The Location of Culture*, 85–92. London: Routledge.

Busoni, Mila. 2000. *Genere, Sesso, Cultura*. Rome: Carocci.

Caponetto, Rosetta Giuliani. 2021. "Fear and Nostalgia in Italian Studies." In *Diversity in Italian Studies*, edited by Siân Gibby and Anthony Julian Tamburri. New York: John Calandra Italian American Institute.

Coffin, William Sloane. 1997. *A Passion for the Possible*. New York: Knox.

Coleman, Nancy. 2020. "Why We're Capitalizing Black." *New York Times*, July 5. https://www.nytimes.com/2020/07/05/insider /capitalized-black.html

Crenshaw, Kimberlé. 2016. "The Urgency of Intersectionality." TED video. https://www.ted.com/talks/kimberle_crenshaw_the _urgency_of_intersectionality/up-next.

Du Bois, W. E. B. 1899. *The Philadelphia Negro: A Social Study.* Philadelphia: University of Pennsylvania Press.

Eddo-Lodge, Reni. 2017. *Why I'm No Longer Talking to White People about Race.* London: Bloomsbury.

Essed, Philomena. 1990. *Everyday Racism: Reports from Women of Two Cultures.* Alameda, CA: Hunter House.

Fabietti, Ugo. 1995. *L'identità etnica. Storia e critica di un concetto equivoco.* Rome: La Nuova Italia Scientifica.

Faloppa, Federico. 2011. *Razzisti a parole (per tacer dei fatti).* Rome: Laterza.

Fanon, Frantz. 1952. *Peau noire, masques blancs.* Paris: Les Éditions du Seuil. Translated by Richard Philcox as *Black Skin, White Masks.* New York: Grove Press, 1967.

Gallini, Clara. 1991. "Giochi Pericolosi. Dall'esotismo al razzismo in alcune pratiche simboliche." In *Problemi del socialismo* 2, 149–170.

Gallisot, René, and Annamaria Rivera. 1997. L'imbroglio etnico. Bari: Edizioni Dedalo.

Gallotti, Cecilia, and Marcello Maneri. 1998. "Elementi di analisi del discorso dei media: lo 'straniero' nella stampa quotidiana." In *Io non sono razzista ma . . . Strumenti per disimparare il razzismo*, edited by Paola Tabet and Silvana Di Bella. Rome: Anicia.

Goldberg, David Theo. 2006. "Racial Europeanization." *Ethnic and Racial Studies* 29 (2): 331–364.

Guevara, Ernesto "Che." [1997] 2000. *The African Dream: The Diaries of the Revolutionary War in the Congo.* Translated by Patrick Camiller. New York: Grove Press.

Guillaumin, Colette. 1972. *L'idéologie raciste: Genèse et langage actuel.* Paris: Mouton. https://www.persee.fr/doc/ierii_1764-8319_1972 _mon_2_1.

Hall, Stuart. 1990. "Cultural Identity and Diaspora." In *Identity: Community, Culture, Difference*, edited by Jonathan Rutherford, 222–237. London: Lawrence & Wishart.

Hawthorne, Camilla. 2019. "Prefazione." In *Future*, edited by Igiaba Scego, 19–32. Florence: Effequ.

Hawthorne, Camilla, and Angelica Pesarini. 2020. "Making Black Lives Matter in Italy: A Transnational Dialogue." Public Books, December 11. https://www.publicbooks.org/making-black-lives -matter-in-italy-a-transnational-dialogue/.

hooks, bell. 1990. *Yearning: Race, Gender and Cultural Politics*. Boston: South End Press.

———. 2000. *All about Love: New Visions*. New York: HarperCollins.

Jacobson, Matthew Frye. 1998. *Whiteness of a Different Color: European Immigrants and the Alchemy of Race*. Cambridge, MA: Harvard University Press.

Juteau-Lee, Danielle. 1995. "Introduction: (Re)constructing the Categories of 'Race' and 'Sex': The Work of a Precursor." In *Racism, Sexism, Power and Ideology*, by Colette Guillaumin, 1–26. London: Routledge.

"La vérité en face avec (Kemi Seba) du dimanche 26 décembre 2021—équinoxe TV." 2021. YouTube video, December 26. https://www.youtube.com/watch?v=rBhMGDuoHMY.

Lombardi-Diop, Cristina, and Caterina Romeo. 2012. "Paradigms of Postcoloniality in Contemporary Italy." In *Postcolonial Italy: Challenging National Homogeneity*, edited by Cristina Lombardi-Diop and Caterina Romeo, 1–29. New York: Palgrave Macmillan.

Matera, Vincenzo. 1996. *Raccontare gli altri: lo sguardo e la scrittura nei libri di viaggio e nella letteratura etnografica*. Lecce: Argo.

Mathieu, Nicole-Claude. 1985. "Femmes, matière à penser . . . et à reprodui re." In *L'Arraisonnement des femmes. Essais en Anthropologie des sexes*, edited by Nicole-Claude Mathieu. Paris: Edition de l'EHESS. Kindle.

Möschel, Mathias. 2011. "Race in Mainland European Legal Analysis: Towards a European Critical Race Theory." *Ethnic and Racial Studies* 34 (10): 1648–1664.

Ngũgĩ wa Thiong'o. 1986. *Decolonising the Mind: The Politics of Language in African Literature*. London: James Currey.

Nzegwu, Nkiru. 2003. "Sisterhood." In *African Women and Feminism: Reflecting on the Politics of Sisterhood*, edited by Oyèrónké Oyĕwùmi, 7–8. Trenton, NJ: Africa World Press.

Ortiz, Fernando. [1946] 1975. *El engaño de las razas*. Havana: Editorial de ciencias sociales.

Palmer, Brian. 2010. "When Did the Word Negro Become a Taboo?" *Slate*, January 11. https://slate.com/news-and-politics/2010/01/how-old-was-harry-reid-when-the-word-negro-became-taboo.html.

Remotti, Francesco. 1990. *Noi Primitivi*. Torino: Bollati Boringhieri.

Scacchi, Anna. 2012. "Negro, nero, di colore o magari abbronzato: la razza in traduzione." In *Parlare di razza: la linea del colore tra Italia e Stati Uniti*, edited by Tatiana Petrovich Njegosh and Anna Scacchi, 254–284. Verona: Ombre Corte.

Schneider, Jane. 1998. *Italy's Southern Question: Orientalism in One Country*. Oxford: Berg.

Steinmetz, Katy. 2020. "She Coined the Term 'Intersectionality' over 30 Years Ago. Here's What It Means to Her Today." Interview by Kimberlé Crenshaw. *Time*, February 20. https://time.com/5786710/kimberle-crenshaw-intersectionality/.

Tabet, Paola. 1997. *La pelle giusta*. Torino: Einaudi.

———. 1998. "Introduction." In *Io non sono razzista ma . . . Strumenti per disimparare il razzismo*, edited by Paola Tabet and Silvana Di Bella, 7–17. Rome: Anicia.

Taylor, Bridie. 2019. "Intersectionality 101: What Is It and Why Is It Important?" Womankind Worldwide, November 24. https://www.womankind.org.uk/intersectionality-101-what-is-it-and-why-is-it-important/.

Tutu, Desmond. 1999. *No Future without Forgiveness*. New York: Image Doubleday.

van Dijk, Teun Adrianus. 1984. *Prejudice in Discourse. An Analysis of Ethnic Prejudice in Cognition and Conversation*. Amsterdam: John Benjamins.

X, Malcolm, and Alex Haley. [1965] 1992. *The Autobiography of Malcolm X: As Told to Alex Haley*. New York: Ballantine Books.

Notes on Contributors

GENEVIÈVE MAKAPING is an adjunct professor in French language and culture at the University of Mantova and has taught English at the high school level in Mantova and the Province of Mantova since 2013. She was born in Cameroon and has lived in Italy since 1982. She received a PhD in Multimedia Educational Technology and Communication Studies from the University of Calabria, where she taught Cultural Anthropology in the Department of Political Science for thirteen years. She was the first Black editor of an Italian daily newspaper, *La Provincia cosentina* (2004–2007), and of a television channel, Metrosat (2004–2010). She is the protagonist of the documentary *Maka*, directed by Elia Moutamid and written by Simone Brioni with Moutamid.

SIMONE BRIONI is an associate professor in the Department of English at Stony Brook University and affiliated faculty in the Department of Africana Studies and the Department of Women's, Gender, and Sexuality Studies. His research focuses on the literary and cinematographic representation and self-representation of migrants. He has edited Shirin Ramzanali Fazel's *Islam and Me: Narrating the Diaspora*

(Rutgers University Press, 2023), which is included in the Other Voices of Italy series.

VICTORIA OFFREDI POLETTO (senior lecturer emerita) and GIOVANNA BELLESIA CONTUZZI (professor and chair) have taught and collaborated in the Department of Italian Studies at Smith College since 1990. They are committed to bringing the voices of migrant and second-generation women writers to the English-speaking world. In addition to Geneviève Makaping's *Reversing the Gaze: What If the Other Were You?*, together they have translated many short stories from Italian into English as well as four other books: Adrián N. Bravi's *My Language Is a Jealous Lover* (Rutgers University Press, 2023), Gabriella Ghermandi's *Queen of Flowers and Pearls*, Cristina Ali Farah's *Little Mother*, and Dacia Maraini's *Stowaway on Board*.